# Faaltugiri

## and other flashbacks

HOW I SURVIVED A CHILDHOOD IN THE '80S

Janhavi Samant

Illustrations by

Abhilasha S. Khatri

**Disclaimer**

**This book is a work of fact.
Any resemblance to characters and incidents in real life is purely deliberate.**



Printed in India

IndiePress

ISBN: 978-93-6045-007-6

Second Printing, 2025

IndiePress

A division of Nasadiya Technologies Private Ltd.

Koramangala, Bangalore

Karnataka-560029

http://indiepress.in/

Edited by Shikha Lal

Cover Design by Dhanashari Ubhayakar

Book Design by Yogita Mhatre

Publishing Consultant : Souvik Bhattacharjee

# Advance Reviews

'Funny and brisk, this memoir is like a pomegranate, bursting with flavour. Light and yet deep in unexpected ways.'

***Aakar Patel***

'In *Faaltugiri and Other Flashbacks*, Janhavi Samant takes us on a delightful trip down nostalgia lane, peppered with anecdotes, insights and poignant details only those who grew up in '80s and '90s Bombay would get. Witty, fun and unsparing, by revisiting her childhood, the author manages to make the reader revisit their own, with both nostalgia and empathy.'

***Kiran Manral***

'An engaging memoir set in the vibrant diversity of 1980s' Bombay.'

***Moni Mohsin***

'Full of the *bhankas*, *dildaari*, comradeship and everyday élan of a city that felt like a casual film set, with everyone deciding on their own characters, their unique *ishtyle*, brio and élan, these are easy-going stories of a distinctly Bombay childhood.'

***Paromita Vohra***

'A hilarious and heartwarming memoir of Bombay childhood in the '80s. An entire generation that grew up on Doordarshan and Jeetendra movies will relate to Janhavi's rib-tickling life story.'

***Vir Sanghvi***

# The Beginning

I was brought to 1, Loukik when I was three months old. My parents – Chitra and Vasant, who will hereafter be termed as Aai and Baba – had left my Baba's joint family in a huff after yet another argument and arrived at this poky Dadar East flat. It was 1977.

Baban kaka, our *istriwala*, who ran his shop right outside our living room window, tells me that before proceeding to unlock the door to our new flat, my dad first plonked my tiny form on a heap of crumpled clothes in his shop. I must have scrunched up my face and rolled my eyes to tune in to the onslaught of noise and sights around this new place – crows cawing raucously, an out-of-tune train horn tooting desultorily as it stopped at the nearby Dadar station, a carpenter somewhere close by sawing vigorously, perhaps an *azaan* from the masjid nearby and the presence of half-a-dozen strangers loitering about at this small shop. Such a difference it must have been from the sleepy lanes of my grandmother's Shivaji Park residence or the quiet neighbourhood of my dad's house in Kamgar Nagar, Kurla, where I lived before. Baban kaka must have clicked his fingers in front of my face or whistled softly so that my twinkling eyes met his.

An instant connection – with Baban kaka and the noisy new world of Loukik neighbourhood – was made. So much so that, over the years, Baban kaka ended up as a quasi-babysitter for me and I ended up heavily influenced by his love for trashy cinema and Hindi film songs.

The world was quite a different place then. In those days, women asked for extra plastic bags from shopkeepers and saved gift wrappers under their mattresses to reuse when needed. Kumar Gaurav used to be a heartthrob. For some reason, moisturisers and fairness creams were called vanishing creams.

Parenting was a completely different ballgame back then. Parents didn't feel the need for phonics and extra-curricular classes or television to flood their children's time with. Most of them just delivered children, perhaps gave them a rupee or two to hire a bicycle in the vacations or eat pepsicola (popsicles) and dismissed them to a life of extreme inactivity and boredom. No one bothered about security or child safety. I was sent out to buy coriander, sliced bread and cigarettes from hawkers since I was four years of age and walked alone to school when I was six. It wouldn't be an exaggeration to say that kids were the least important factor in the family's hierarchy of priorities.

Life, in general, was quite dull. The days used to be long, sunny and slow. Kids didn't have much to do, except think up silly ideas to entertain themselves. Sometimes I played with my mum's dupatta, posing in front of the mirror, pretending I was a film star. Sometimes I ran barefoot in my white cotton petticoat, along with the other kids on the street, behind the municipal corporation person who came to fumigate the gutters in our gully with his loud droning machine. Else, we would run behind open jeeps to leap and hang onto the rear door when the vehicle slowed down.

In the peak of summer, we would stand in the heat and argue over what to play. Hours were spent in figuring if we should play 'London, London, Stop!' or 'Fire on the Mountain! Run, Run, Run!' or '*Sakhali*' or '*Aaabadubi*'. We had no fancy summer camps to attend. Instead, our fine motor skills were developed crushing leaves from plants to make fake bhaji and collecting *choora* from scraping erasers, sharpening pencils or thermocol and storing them in pencil boxes, which our mums would discover months later and throw out without our permission.

Our gross motor skills were developed while walking backwards or with the eyes closed on the way home from school. We played and we played, outdoors under the blazing sun, till we turned red in the face and sweat slowly trickled from the back of our heads, down our spines and into our bloomer *chaddis*. We played till our knees and shins were grazed from falling over the harsh uneven concrete of our building compound. Boredom was such a way of life that we did some random things to entertain ourselves. Sometimes we would walk with our chappals in our hands; sometimes we would sharpen our fingers in the sharpener (if you put your finger into a sharpener and turn it skilfully, it will gently remove the outer layer of your skin and nail; sometimes, though, it'll take away much of your nail and skin and hurt like hell!).

At times we put stones or leftover chapatis from the lunchbox through people's letter boxes!

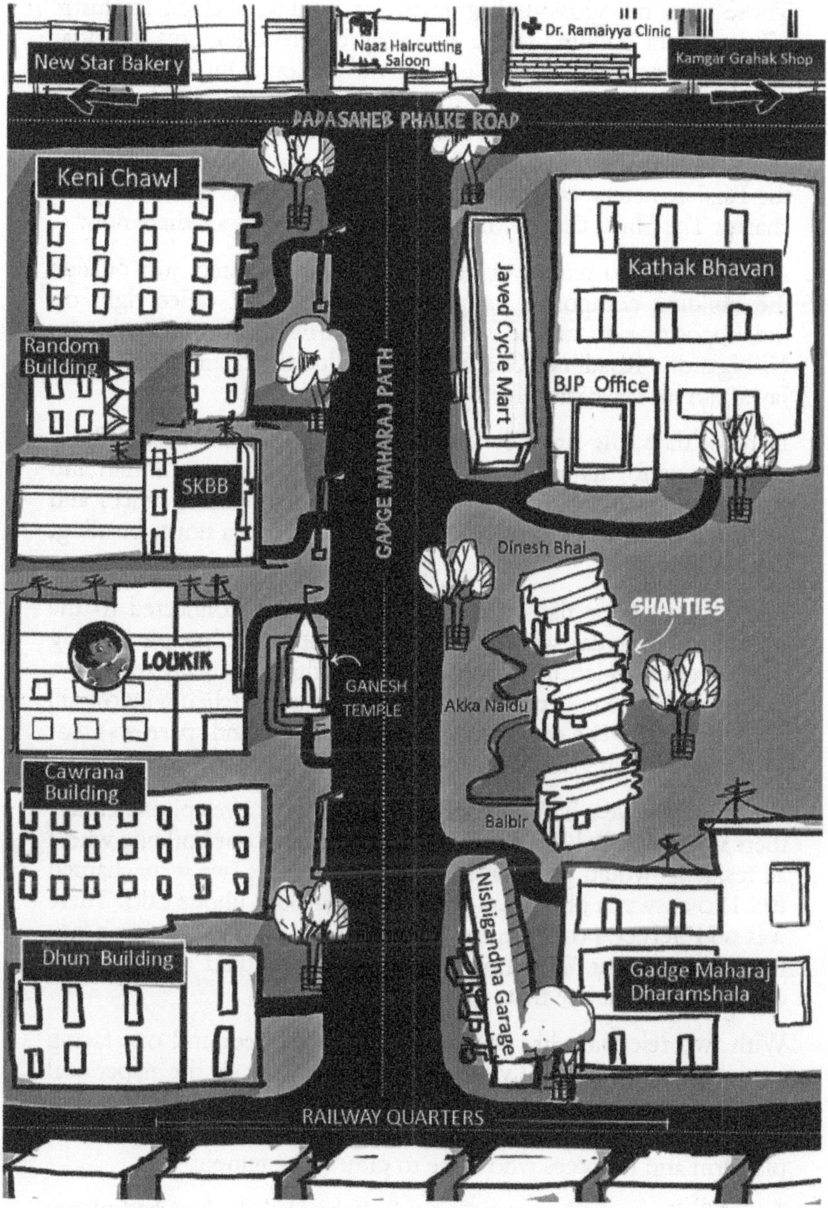
New Star Bakery
Naaz Haircutting Saloon
Dr. Ramaiyya Clinic
Kamgar Grahak Shop
DADASAHEB PHALKE ROAD
Keni Chawl
Javed Cycle Mart
Kathak Bhavan
Random Building
BJP Office
GADGE MAHARAJ PATH
SKBB
Dinesh Bhai
SHANTIES
LOUKIK
GANESH TEMPLE
Akka Naidu
Cawrana Building
Balbir
Nishigandha Garage
Dhun Building
Gadge Maharaj Dharamshala
RAILWAY QUARTERS

Those were my glorious beginnings at Loukik, a plain, lacklustre 17-apartment building facing a rather grey, green-less area in Dadar East, right near the busiest part of the station. Our building was flanked by a couple of old-world Parsi buildings and the Dadar Railway quarters on one side and two old-world chawls on the other. It is said that the plot facing Loukik was once a Tower of Silence; the Parsi cemetery was then razed and the land was given away for charity. The Shree Gadge Maharaj Dharamshala stands there now.

A small Ganesha temple stands right at our doorstep, just outside the building compound *katta*, and the BJP head office right on the opposite side of the street. The Nalawade brothers ran the Nishigandha Roadlines Garage right outside the dharamshala while Javed ran his cycle shop further down the same side.

In those days, the late '70s and early '80s, Dadasaheb Phalke Road was famous for its film studios (Rooptara, Shree Cine Sound and Ranjit Studio and a thriving Junior Artists Association office) and its textile mills (Gulmohur and Tata Mills). It was a noisy, bustling, vibrant locality.

Our ground floor flat overlooked the lane that connected to the station and everyday we would see a steady stream of people walking to and from the platform. We had sparrows chirping shrilly and crows cawing rudely to collect chapati pieces from our kitchen window sill every morning. The only birds (other than crows and sparrows) that I have seen are in Hindi films.

We did not have a TV at home. We didn't have a telephone either; there was only one household with a telephone in our building where all residents would go to answer their phone calls (we were charged Re. 1 to answer a phone call and Rs. 3 to make a phone call). There was no Internet, no smartphone, no YouTube and yet we didn't lack for entertainment. The Loukik neighbourhood had a buzz of its own. It was built like that.

With two television-like windows facing the street and one facing an *istriwala*, we got a live feed of pretty much all the hyperlocal entertainment and news updates we needed at the time. People kept pouring onto our small street – passengers from the railway station platform and devotees who came to pray at the temple.

Lots of idle gossip happened as well. Baban kaka's shop had plenty of hangers-on – film extras looking for work, maids whiling away time in between different households, servants on the way from the grocers' or waiting for clothes to be pressed, and chawl residents catching up.

Residents of the Shri Krishna Chawl would eat, drink and socialise on the footpaths of their chawl next door while Akka Naidu's family of errant husband and eight children often spilled out of their single room shanty across our home. They peed, fought, played right on the footpath.

Even if one didn't go around looking for it, gully gossip reached everyone. Roadside Romeos from the chawls wooed fair maidens from either Loukik or the Parsi buildings. Balbir crooned '*Dekho maine dekha hai ye ek sapna*' or '*Yeh ladki zarasi deewani lagti hai*' whenever Kalika, the first floor Ajgaonkar's niece, left home to buy sliced bread. For some strange reason, everyone in the gully knew about the *chakkar* between Mukherjee's son and a Parsi girl (name withheld) from Cawrana building, except her own mother. Her cousin would raise her skirt a couple of notches between stepping out of her building and getting onto the street when going to college. It was all for the benefit of someone in Kathak Bhavan they say.

Love blossomed in our gully's nooks. I remember this one time when the puny good-for-nothing Sudhir from Sri Krishna Building asked me to hand over an anonymous love letter to Golda Prabhu on the third floor.

It isn't a terribly good idea to hire a four-year-old girl to post a secret letter. I'll tell you why. I screwed up by handing over the letter to Golda's mother instead. To make things worse, when Prabhu kaki widened her eyes in anger, I quickly revealed the sender's name and then got screwed myself because the Prabhus immediately complained to my mother. Needless to say, I got soundly whacked for getting involved!

Of course, I didn't learn my lesson. I again delivered an oral message meant for the beautiful Kalika from Balbir to her aunt Mrs. Ajgaonkar! This time too I got whacked – by Mrs. Ajgaonkar first and then my own mother. In those days, if we complained of some neighbour hitting us, our parents would simply assume that it must have been our fault and give us one more whack just for getting into trouble.

Then of course there were the characters in my own house.

My dad was a dentist and there was always a constant stream of people – mechanics, cycle *shopwalas*, tailors, maids, labourers, clerks, mill workers – at our house. Some came to seek medicines for loose motions or fever, some to get a letter written in English, some actually came to get their teeth extracted at home. But most of all, people came because my parents helped anyone who landed at their doorstep.

A few drunkards in our gully added to its charm. Every once in a while, the gully drunkard Mhadya would arrive sloshed, staggering to the temple at our doorstep, around 10 p.m. or so.

Mhadya: Bhe$^%%, come out.

It was not quite clear whom he was asking to come out, so nobody did.

Mhadya: Ma#%&, I told you na, come out. If you have *himmat* (courage), come out.

Same lack of response.

Mhadya: Arre... (moving on to drunken slurring)

Then out of steam for a bit and again...

Mhadya: M#^%@^, Ch^#&^, Bh#%^^&^%, come out!

My father would then open the door. It was Baba's nature to routinely get into things that didn't in the slightest involve him.

Baba: Bh%&^^ Mhadya, get lost. You have drunk too much today.

Mhadya (stumped now that someone had actually come out): Sorry, Doctor. Sorry, Doctor. I am going, going, going.

Our *dudhwali* Aaji (a 65-year-old homeless grandmother who slept on the street and who delivered milk to residents) was also a drunkard. Sometimes she would throw a drunken tantrum right at our doorstep. She was a thin, dark, old woman with a head full of white hair and two teeth jutting out in the front.

For some reason, when she drank too much, she'd come, stinking of country liquor and sit at our doorstep to chat with us. After a while, she would start blabbering, which would make us giggle. And Baba would say, "*Aaj gaadi fast hai lagta hai.*" (Someone seems very drunk today.)

Clearly, it was an unconventional childhood; we met and loitered with a lot of unsavoury characters. 'Baby' they called me fondly. They would ruffle my hair, place a chocolate in my hand and pat my back. If I strayed too far from the house towards the street, someone would sternly pack me off home. Instead of 'Johny Johny', Baban kaka taught me '*Jaanu meri jaan*'.

For a while, we even had house help in the form of the 55-year-old Dada to take care of me when I was three or four years old. Dada was addicted to playing *matka* (gambling) and often took me for a game or two on the way back from the vegetable market. I loved it because if he won, Dada bought me a Five Star, calling me his lucky charm. Of course, my mum freaked out when she found out and sacked him immediately.

It was a strange upbringing. We didn't take any vacations or have a family native place to escape to every summer. I am a complete city bird. Greenery and silence make me uncomfortable. I find breathing petrol-laced smoke entirely natural. I need temple bell clamour, enthusiastic noisy *aartis* and train horns to tell me that all's right with the world.

I had parents who were stingy with money but generous to a fault with everything else. We were privileged, but in terms of education and experience rather than riches; we were happy, but due to our intent rather than circumstances. I had a voice, an opinion, the freedom to dissent in our family, although I got whacked for it pretty often too.

Our world view was different.

'*Faaltugiri* and Other Flashbacks' is a unique perspective of childhood in the '80s. It's also a unique view of Bombay (now Mumbai) and its people – not from its fancy flyovers or from its filthy slums, not from the *ittar*-laden gullies of Bhendi Bazaar or the elegance of Fort, but somewhere in between all that gloss. It is all about a place full of real people who fought in smelly staircases, who cried and threw tantrums in public, who slept on the footpath but with dignity, who tried and failed, but who had great stories to tell.

This book is a peep into a life, places and institutions – City Video library, Garibi Hatao Tailors, Rooptara Studios, Ranjit Studio, Gupta Soaps, Naaz Haircutting Saloon – which now exist only in that ordinary eight-year-old's memory.

'*Faaltugiri* and Other Flashbacks' is an attempt to keep these people and places and that kind of unconventional childhood alive in our minds.

# 1.

# Samant vs Samant

If you were to begin at the very beginning, the most crucial ingredients of my unconventional childhood were my parents, Vasant and Chitra – Baba and Aai, of course. Till the time I became a parent and started showing the same crazy characteristics, I was convinced they were not my real parents.

To be honest, most parents of the early '80s were similarly villain-like. With most of them finding newfound freedom from the joint-family fold, seeing many married women getting into the workforce, facing babysitting issues, being extremely consciousness about financial security, conforming to social and religious duties and despite all that, being budget conscious in everything, most of us had rigid, extremely pushy parents, who viewed single-minded focus on academics and settling down as the only route to success. But I realised very early in life that my parents were more mental than most.

They were both fiercely outspoken and opinionated about everything from world politics to each other's families. As a result of this conditioning, I learnt never to tire or be scared of loud arguments, confrontations and badmouthing. They both believed that they knew the best about everything. Despite these similarities, they did not get along with each other and made a career out of bringing out the worst in each other.

The story of how they landed up at 1, Loukik is also rooted in their outspokenness. Vasant met Chitra as a prospective groom through a meeting arranged by relatives. Chitra was an aspiring light classical singer, a graduate, extremely beautiful, and her broad-minded family wanted an educated husband who would allow her to sing and work after marriage. Vasant had also graduated as a dentist on scholarship, practised in a government hospital and had just started a clinic in Vasai. It was considered to be a fair match by all, even if the groom and his father were known to be Communists (for some reason, it was always said with dread and shock).

So one evening, Vasant went to see Chitra at her Shivaji Park residence. When Chitra's father mentioned her singing, Vasant immediately asked:

Vasant: She sings? (To Chitra) You sing?

Chitra (with her eyes downcast): Yes.

Vasant: Can you sing '*Rulake gaya sapna mera*' from *Jewel Thief*? Now?

Chitra (a little perplexed): Yes, I can.

She sang that song, every note intact. And there, Vasant made up his mind. He immediately conveyed his interest in the proposal along with the request that the marriage would only be registered and no money or grand gestures were to be exchanged during this wedding. "Both parties will come empty-handed to the registered marriage," specified Vasant. My grandfather thought it was all very convenient. To have a son-in-law not demanding anything was rare in those days.

He was shocked, of course, to find out that when Vasant said empty-handed, he actually meant empty-handed! There was not even a *mangalsutra* for the bride! A *mangalsutra* was arranged last minute by Vasant's sister-in-law, Bharti. And finally, Chitra went home to the Samant household in Kamgar Nagar with Vasant.

In all the urgency and excitement of finding a dentist catch for Chitra, not a single person – including Chitra herself – had wondered about how the emancipated bride would fit into Vasant's strictly patriarchal family setup, with two sisters-in-law (one married with her family and one still unmarried then), a brother as well as his family already in residence.

Chitra walked into her marital home with a transistor; the only time she didn't listen to music was when she sang herself. Samant family members spoke in low volumes; Chitra spoke excitedly in high decibels. Nana was quite a disciplinarian; he didn't approve of TV or films or, as Chitra discovered, even film music.

1 LOUKIK

The first evening Nana came home to find the radio playing in his house, he asked testily, "Why is this house sounding like Ram Bharose Hindu Hotel? Put that off." The first time Chitra spoke to him directly, he responded, "Haven't your parents taught you to speak softly?"

Vasant's incessant argumentativeness anyway got on Nana's nerves. So did Chitra's outspokenness. Needless to say, the couple got thrown out of the household within a couple of years. A room was quickly vacated by the tenants of my maternal grandfather's 1-BHK flat in Loukik for the couple to settle in. The couple had just had a baby. That baby was me.

It was easy to tell that my parents were not like other parents. My mother never deferred to my dad. She was not coy, she wore skirts and jeans, she worked for a government organisation, and after that, she attended singing classes. She didn't mince her words if she had to disagree with anybody. She aspired to be a light classical singer and a *sangeet natak* actress and, although not wildly famous, has been fairly successful at what she did.

My dentist dad was not meek either. He read a lot and he questioned a lot. He cooked, he drank alcohol, he smoked religiously. He even sent me to the *paanwala* round the corner to buy his cigarettes! He argued over the country's politics in nobody's favour; he picked fights with bus conductors for being obstructive with other passengers; he argued with my school teachers. He got into fistfights at times but was known to be gentle with his patients.

Both my parents didn't follow any religion or rituals. It is said that when the Ganeshotsav organisers came home to ask for a donation, Baba drove them away, saying, "I am a Hindu because of an accident of birth. I have not chosen this religion!"

Clearly, my parents had very strange ideas about life. They were both creatures of habit. They never bunked work. They only ever ate chapatis dipped in chai for breakfast. *Poha* or *upma* was only meant for the occasion when guests stayed over. We never dined out and when we did go out to snack, it was strictly local – either Shivaji Park Gymkhana canteen to eat batata vada and drink Energee, or Farmer Brothers to eat chicken *pattice*, pastry and lassi. We were never asked what we wanted to eat. We always ordered the same things.

If I asked for money to have sev puri, my mum would say that she'd make it for me at home. A) It didn't taste the same. Aai's sev-paani puri always tasted tame and well, non-*bhaiyya* like. B) When one eats out, the point is to eat *out*. It's fun to pop a big puri in your mouth as a car whizzes by or as a horse gallops past at Chowpatty. It's about walking in the rush at Dadar TT and then letting the smell of frying patties lure you to eat a *ragda-pattice*. It's about impulse, fun. It's about not having to serve or clear the table. But Aai never understood this.

Like other parents, my parents didn't aspire for riches. Neither were they ever impressed by wealth. They never dreamt of owning a house or car or buying land or did what other normal parents were doing to ensure financial security. My father didn't own a home till he died! They didn't work harder to make more money. But they were big on saving.

For instance, if brand A costs Rs. 60 and brand B costs Rs. 80, they'd automatically assume that brand B was exploiting its customer by over-charging. It'd never occur to either of them that perhaps B would last longer or looked better than A. They also had a pathological problem with spending money.

Let me give an example:

Say, a tap leaked and a plumber was called to repair it. The following would transpire:

Plumber: We need to change the *vicer* (that's what he called the 'washer', a crucial part of a tap). It'll cost (say) Rs. 10.

Baba (with his eyes wide in disbelief): Whaaaaat? You can get a *vicer* for Rs. 2.

Mind you, this was not haggling.

Plumber (laughingly): Fine, you buy the *vicer* and I'll fix it.

Which meant that I'd be dispatched to the nearby Shindewadi to scour shops for a Rs-2 washer. The cheapest washer would cost Rs. 7. But my father would have given me only Rs. 2 because he really believed that that was its price. And so I'd have to go back home empty-handed.

Baba: Did you get it?

Me: Baba, it costs Rs. 7. Nothing is cheaper than that.

Baba (triumphantly handing me Rs. 5 more): See? I told you it's not Rs. 10. The man would have cheated us. Go and buy it.

Our lives were full of such worthless ventures. Finding door handles, stoppers, wires, bulb-holders, hinges, curtain hooks, my parents would trudge all over Dadar West, checking shop after shop for bargains on thoroughly inconsequential items. My mother walked to Plaza Cinema market because vegetables were cheaper there. She'd return huffing and puffing, laden with ten kilos of vegetables, feeling proud of herself.

My parents thought of money as a means to itself, not for the things or convenience it could afford. They were not stingy, mind you. They just had a weird ethos for spending.

They would fight with a grocer for Rs. 2 but would let a carpenter get off lightly for taking three months to make two diwans and screwing up an entire piece of furniture, saying, "Let it be." Once when we had a storage space crunch, my parents commissioned a carpenter to remake our furniture – to extend the existing living room showcase into a wall-to-wall unit. The carpenter literally cut the existing showcase vertically right in the middle and stacked the rear half on top of the front half. This, of course, made for a wall-full of drawers but with a depth of only seven inches.

My parents never realised what a con this was until they noticed that they couldn't store anything in it! We had to roll up ironed clothes like jalebis to fit them into those shelves and mum's harmonium had to find a new shelter. Yet, the carpenter got full payment because he was a 'poor man' and the showcase wasn't replaced for more than a decade.

Aai-Baba didn't believe in leisure travel. We must have had three pleasure trips – twice to Pune to Appa kaka's (my father's elder brother) place and once to Nasik to Kasturi aatya's (my dad's younger sister) place – as a family in 20 years. The first time I sat in a long-distance train with my family was when I was 29 and we were leaving for my wedding in Cochin.

They didn't believe in idle eating; they didn't buy Bourbon biscuits or potato chips or ketchup because we ate too many of them too soon. They didn't buy Parle-G or Marie biscuits because we didn't eat them and they would lie around getting soft. We weren't bought toys, like an aeroplane or a doll or cars, because we either broke or disfigured them.

To be fair, people didn't really buy toys in those days, at least for their own children anyway. I once asked my father why they didn't buy us any toys. My father replied, "Why do you need toys? You have a younger sister. Play with her."

I first saw a Barbie when Babi maushi (my grandmum's youngest sister who lived in the US) brought it for my sister. My father scoffed at our excitement saying, "Huh, they've put her in such fancy clothes. Why haven't they given her a *chaddi*?"

We were bought school uniforms that were three sizes bigger and wore them right until they were discoloured and our teachers urged us to buy new ones. We'd wear school shoes till our toes burst through in mute protest. And if the shoe gave way in January or so, my parents would refuse to buy me new ones till the start of the next year in June!

Baba: Oh it's just two months for your vacations now. Your foot will grow again. May as well buy them in June.

Me: But our teacher keeps asking me why I am always dressed in civil shoes. And I can't give that excuse na? They ask for a note. Otherwise they punish us.

Baba: Okay. I will give a note.

The note said that my father was sorry that I had outgrown my shoes but he was unable to afford new shoes till the next year and that he hoped that the teacher would be patient! If you quibbled too much, he'd retort, "Count yourself lucky. I didn't have any chappals till my first day in college. Even those were secondhand."

They were never apologetic about saying that they couldn't afford things. And they did it in a way that put people's noses out of joints. At parents' meetings, Baba would say things like, "We can't afford donations like this. Do you think we earn black money to fritter it away like this?" Needless to say, it caused many business family parents to blush in shame. And all this to protest a donation of Rs. 10!

As a child, I imagined that most households were loving peaceful havens, where people spoke softly and lovingly to each other. All except mine. In our home, conflict was the only constant. Argument was the family's driving force and sarcasm its fuel. It wasn't their fault. Their view of life was itself a bit skewed. And boy, did they argue.

Once my parents got conned into going for one of those Club Mahindra type early timeshare presentations. The salesperson asked them what they would drink. My mum asked for a cold drink; my dad asked for a chai. They had one of their most memorable arguments after this event. On their return:

Aai: Arre, why did you order chai? You should have ordered a cold drink.

Baba: I wanted a chai, that's why.

Aai: Chai you get at home. You won't get a cold drink at home.

Baba: So what? I wanted a chai.

Aai: Chai costs Rs. 5 and a cold drink Rs. 12.

Baba: What nonsense you talk. The Nerurkars (my mum's side of the family, of course) must be doing this sort of thing.

Aai: You are nonsensical. Ha ha, as if the Samants are all born Nawabs only.

Suppose someone from my mum's side of the family gifted us a bedsheet set:

Baba: Shee, what is this? It's so garish.

Aai: At least my side of the family gives something, unlike yours.

If I came home with good results in any subject:

Me: Baba, I scored 22 out of 25 in History/English/Science.

Baba: Arre wah, very good. Go, show your mother. Nobody in Nerurkar *khaandaan* must have scored that high ever.

Suppose I couldn't get a maths sum right:

Baba (ensuring Aai was within earshot): It's not your fault. Your Aai's full *khaandaan* couldn't ever manage maths.

If I was rude:

Aai: This is not you talking. This is your father's rudeness. That full Samant family has no manners.

If I sang a song well:

Aai: See how good it is that you've taken after me. If you'd taken after your father, you wouldn't have been able to string two lines of a song together.

Baba would then take huge offence and immediately sing Kishore Kumar's '*Pal bhar ke liye*' song from Johnny Mera Naam or Mukesh's '*Har dil jo pyaar karega*' in full flow.

Baba loved to drag Anna (my grandfather) into all his arguments while my mum routinely invoked the names of my father's relatives. According to Baba, my grandfather was a loser. (He was, I suppose. He spent a lifetime in inconsequence. He was a lawyer but wildly unsuccessful at it, after which he started a polythene factory in Panvel, which also was loss-making. He then started an electrical trading company called Vishwas Electricals, which didn't do well but at least provided the entire family with tubelights, starters and chokers from the unsold stock for a fair part of a decade.) Baba said that the so-imagined collective dumbness of the Nerurkars was all Anna's fault. My mother, of course, not only refuted this but also did her fair bit in criticising my dad's side of the family. Once they got on their family bitching tirade, the entire argument would spin like a top; it would start at one place and then its own crazy momentum would decide where it'd run out of steam.

And wherever it started, it'd always ended with Baba pointing to his head and scoffing, "Arre, don't give me your *khaandaan* ka big talk. At least I have a full head of hair and will do so till my dying day. Not like you Nerurkars who become bald at 20. Feel lucky you got a handsome husband."

My mother would retort, "Look at your *bhajiya*-like nose. If your daughters had turned out like you, you'd find it difficult to get them married. Then of what use is a head full of hair?"

Of course, it was a thoroughly pointless fight but recurring nonetheless. And other than its entertainment value to the rest of us, it achieved zilch.

Aai-Baba viewed life as if it was a big war and each day had to be conquered. They believed that unless they fought, day in and day out – with *baniyas*, ticket conductors, building neighbours, *cigarettewalas*, beggars, teachers, principals – people would take advantage of them.

They believed that the only way to deal with problems was to confront them head on. My parents even sorted out their social problems like that – with full-on aggression.

So while our neighbours sneakily slit our scooter seats because my father protested against parking charges, my parents just rushed in headlong with all guns blazing, whether it was shouting at our top-floor neighbour to protest his throwing water out from the balcony or stomping to the *baniya* to fight for over-charging us 5 paise or for handing out a toffee instead of 10-paise change.

For instance, once I came home from the *kirana* store with 10 paise less in change.

Baba: Arre, sliced bread costs only Rs. 2.05. You should have brought back Rs. 2.95. He's given you only Rs. 2.85. Didn't you count?

Me: No, no. That shopkeeper said…

Baba (all worked up, already spoiling for a fight): What did he say? He's cheated you. He thinks he can get away with this kind of thing.

Me: He said... tell Doctor that…

Baba (cutting me short): He doesn't know what he's doing. *Chal*, let's go to him. I'll show him never to fool around with us anymore. (Rushing to wear his slippers and stepping out of the home, dragging me behind him.)

At the shop, Baba (in a confrontational tone and threatening body language): *Kya re, saale?* How dare you give 10 paise less in change to my daughter? I never thought you'd take advantage of children like that.

*Dukandaar:* Arre doctor, I have not given less money. The price of Wibs has gone up by 10 paise. I told her… (then glaring at me) Aye, didn't I tell you?

Before I could answer, Baba (angrily to me): Why didn't you tell me?

Me (loudly in protest): I tried telling you! You didn't let me finish.

Baba: Okay, okay. No need to shout now. Here, take one jeera *goli*.

As a child, I ate a lot of jeera *golis*. I envied children with sensible parents who measured their words, who lived planned, controlled lives and households. We had chaos at ours. Master procrastinators, my parents. Conked off bulbs or tubelights were never replaced on time. Say, if the bathroom light stopped working, the basin passageway bulb would be stuck into the bathroom while having a bath and then re-fitted in the passage when it was time to brush. And the arrangement would go on for as long as the passageway bulb worked, after which both the bulbs would be replaced at the same time.

When the tape recorder started gurgling, Baba would try his home improvement skills on it with kerosene and cotton swabs. Then when the tape recorder had been further damaged properly, my mum would bring out her small transistor. Then the batteries of the radio would give up. That was the time the first tape recorder went for repair.

TVs usually draw a few gasping breaths or some long shuddering sighs before they crash. My parents never called the ECTV technician. They would shake the set or slap it on the sides, sometimes switching it on and off in quick succession, plugging or unplugging it, till its very last breaths. When the TV finally conked off (even if it was in June and exams were months away), my parents would declare, “Oh good. Now we’ll get it repaired only after your exams.”

My go-with-the-flow, peace-loving personality just continually got on their nerves. I wanted to dream; they wanted to get things done and out of the way. I’d lovingly fold each flap of an umbrella carefully so as to align them together into a nice pattern; my parents would just snap it shut haphazardly.

Aai-Baba walked all over beautiful coloured tiles; I walked on only alternate ones. I loved going by the bus, trundling about, watching the streets and passengers; they wanted the train, all crowded and crammed, just so they could reach on time.

They thought I was too slow. I thought they were too hasty.

Simply speaking, we were just on different wavelengths. My childhood was full of these fluctuating frequencies and crackling static.

2.

# Baba and Bajrangbali

It must be one of my earliest, clearest memories. It was 1981; I must have been four at the time. Cine-mania was high in our part of Dadasaheb Phalke Road back then. Film-viewing wasn't the private I-go-with-my-family-and-sit-in-the-darkness experience it is today. It was a mass, public event. We went in an exodus to the theatres. We went with water, biscuits, wafers, sandwiches, water bottles filled with Rasna, Limlet sweets – basically enough food to survive at least three days in the cinema hall. In the summers, we also took with us handmade fans and cold towels.

And then there were also the times when the cinema theatre came to us. Street screenings were common in Mumbai at the time. During the seven nights of Ganapati and then on some odd festival days like Shivaji or Hanuman Jayanti, at the behest of and due to the benevolence of either local gully leaders Periyarswami Naidu 'Anna' or Dada Padelkar or local music celebrity Nirmal Mukherjee, films would be screened on a large white screen tied between two tall electric poles in our gully too.

These screenings were big social events. The whole street would be in a festive mood; families would finish dinner early. Whichever the film, everyone attended. People trickled out by 8.30 p.m. with their *chaddars* and pillows and staked their claim on the street. Some came with chairs to sit on the footpaths. Loukik residents living on the road-facing side brought their chairs to their balconies; residents from the other side of the building came to the *istriwala's* table in our building compound or sat on the building compound wall.

This is where I saw Amitabh Bachchan in all his glory as Anthony Gonsalves, Mehmood getting up from the dead in *Gumnaam*, Dimple in her swimsuit smooching Rishi Kapoor in *Sagar*, the disturbing molestation in *Ankush* and the outrageous *Fifty Fifty*.

This particular episode happened on a particularly exuberant Hanuman Jayanti. It was an impromptu screening. The street-side notice board outside Chandu Shanbhag's tea stall announced that there would be a film show at around 9 p.m. and suddenly the street was abuzz. The kids were all wound up with excitement and the women muttered slightly because they had to rush through dinner.

Then because it was a special evening and dinner was done, the building gents stepped out for a paan.

Soon everyone caught their seats and the film began. Midway through the film, Baba, who was sitting in a wooden chair right outside our house steps, suddenly collapsed.

"Chitra, my hands and feet have gone numb. I'm dying," he gasped.

Aai panicked, "Vasant, what happened? VASANT?"

By this time, some 30 people sitting nearby, including me, were alerted to this family predicament. Before I could jump down from the compound wall and reach them, some hundred people were already up and around him.

Large-scale pandemonium broke out. By the time I could reach the few steps to our door and see Aai move Baba back home, people had already termed it a heart attack.

Someone shouted, "*Aye, film band karo. Doc ko heart attack aaya hai* (Stop the film. Doc has had a heart attack)." (See, my father was a bit of a celebrity. He fought with everybody over hygiene and civic issues in the street but he was also the local medical advisor. Although he was a dentist – he extracted people's teeth in our dining chair – gully people came to see him for cases of fever, stomach upset, malaria, fits, insulin injections, post-surgery help, second opinion on X-rays and to help judge Ganapati record dance and music competitions and so on.) The screening was stopped.

He was quickly brought into the house. Aai first called my grandmother from Shivaji Park. Some 40 well-meaning people just walked into our home and stood around, handing out advice.

"Try brandy. Does anyone have brandy?"

Someone was summoned to get brandy from someone.

"Press his feet. Hit his back. That will make him feel better."

"Make some sweet chai. Give him chai."

So someone rushed to make chai.

In all this chaos, Baba mutters, "Chitra, my head's really swimming. My feet are becoming numb. My hands are stiff and cold. I'm dying. I'm dying."

More advice followed: "It's paralysis. Make him move his hands and legs, otherwise they will never move. Ever."

So someone held his feet and started rotating them.

"Arre this looks like a fit. Make him smell a chappal."

So then we forced someone's chappal to Baba's nose.

My grandparents entered in a hurry.

Dr. Ramaiyya, who lived on the main street, had been summoned. Dr. Ramaiyya stayed just outside our gully, but he took a really long time to come through the crowd. He was a homeopath and made a living giving insulin and tetanus injections to the locals. He looked a hundred years old and had another hundred-year-old for a compounder, who incidentally looked exactly like music composer Naushad. He walked in authoritatively with Naushad holding the doctor's bag and started his check-up.

Aai: Doctor, he says his hands and feet are going cold.

Baba (in his pained voice): Chitra, get a proper doctor. I may be needing critical care here.

Random onlooker: Doctor, Dr. Ramaiyya is a doctor only. You don't worry.

Baba: Get a proper MBBS doctor. Call Dr. Kotnis.

So someone was dispatched silently to call Dr. Kotnis from the neighbourhood so as to not offend Dr. Ramaiyya.

Ramaiyya (in his comforting tone): Just a second, let me check your eyes and heartbeat till then. What do you feel? Is your stomach hurting?

Baba: No, my stomach isn't hurting. My hands and feet are going cold and numb.

Then while checking Baba's blood pressure, he asked: What have you done all evening? What did you have for dinner?

Baba: The usual. I ate well.

Ramaiyya: Have you had any drink after that?

Baba: No. We just went for a paan and... (and then he suddenly fell sheepishly silent)

Ramaiyya: What happened?

Baba (slowly): The paan was spiked with... with charas.

In that one single moment, all the buzz died. The room went deathly silent.

Baba (with eyes widening in self-realisation): Oh, it's effect of the charas.

Ramaiyya (in his usual mild tone): Have you ever had charas?

Baba: No.

Sriniwas Kashelkar, our neighbour who took my dad along with several others, to the *paanwala* was summoned. "Doctor, I thought you have had charas before. I didn't know this was your first time."

Slowly, people filed out of the home, murmuring, "It was charas. Charas. Doctor had charas", "He'll be okay. It's a kick from charas. Anna, start the film re."

Within six seconds, everyone in the gully knew. Within five minutes, the screening had resumed.

My mother only raised an eyebrow.

Aaji (my grandmother), without considering his present agony, slapped Baba on the back: You irresponsible person. Scaring all of us like that. If you can't handle charas, why did you consume it?

Baba (reverting to old form): If I have never taken it, how will I know?

One more slap on the back.

Aaji: So you were waiting to die to find out? Idiot. What would have happened to my daughter if something had happened to you? Such beautiful daughters you have. Why did you want to do charas anyway?

Baba (sheepishly): Nothing would have happened. Nobody dies because of charas.

One more slap on the arm.

Ramaiyya asked my father to chill and let the trip pass. I think facing my Aaji's ire was already speeding that up.

This episode forever changed the power dynamics at our home.

I knew, of course, that my dad drank, sometimes a little more than he could handle. I knew it was a bad habit. At Arnala, during Ganapati, and at home, when Mukul kaka (his rather degenerate cousin) dropped in, he even played rummy or *teen patti*. I knew that was also a bad habit. Baba also did not follow any religious restrictions of *upvas*, Sankashti or any kind of fasting. He stole plants from the neighbour's gardens in Vasai and Arnala. He stole books also, quite shamelessly.

Although I was too young to know what it actually was, from the hush of the people around, I realised that charas was totally badass. And this happening in front of the whole gully (literally hundreds of people!), I knew that it was scandalous.

Thankfully, nobody remembered any of this the next day. And the only one ribbed was my dad. When he passed, people jokingly asked, "*Kya doctor, paan mangau kya?*" (Doctor, shall we order a paan for you?)

But Baba was also the *gir-gaya-to-bhi-tangdi-upar* types, totally unrepentant. Even if he had lost an argument, morally or otherwise, he'd still insist that he was right and that nobody else had the intellect to understand him. Over the years, he calmly refuted, "It was nothing. I'd have been okay. You guys panicked unnecessarily." And so, though he never admitted his mistake in this episode, this must have been the first time, he actually looked sheepish. That was quite a revelation.

Then there was my Aaji smacking Baba. That vision was too empowering. I learned then that nothing was above Aaji in the family system, that even my Baba could be punished.

As for family politics, I realised in the later years, Aai had discovered the ultimate put-down for Baba. This event was recalled every time Baba tried to act oversmart with her. There were several things the couple didn't forgive each other. These things were routinely culled out to balance everyday arguments.

For instance, Baba couldn't forgive Aai that she cleared her Inter exams without opting for Maths. According to him, only people with zero IQ opted out of a simple subject like maths. Baba never forgave her for never getting a dosa right. Aai never forgave him for keeping her waiting at D Damodar Halwai shop for two hours while he stood waiting for her at Chandu Halwai shop across the street. The charas event was one that Aai kept bringing up every time she was on the losing side of an argument.

Baba, I am afraid, could never get a one-up after that.

# 3.

# The Scooter with a Sidecar

A vehicle is always such a status symbol. It is the best way to show people that one's family is now settled and moving up in life. My parents weren't really that status conscious but they had settled down, or so it seemed, and they somehow felt the need to announce it aloud.

I was around five years or so. Cars weren't much of a necessity then. Aai worked in Wadala, a 15-minute walk from home. Baba worked in Sion, 20 minutes by bus in those days. The only place we regularly went to was my Anna-Aaji's home in Shivaji Park, also a 15-minute walk. We visited Sucheta maushi in Grant Road say, once every two months. We went to Mothi kaki's in Goregaon thrice a year (the first day of Diwali, the first day of Ganapati and once for a week or fortnight's stay during the vacations).

Because of babysitting problems during vacations, I was packed off to Bharti kaki's in Vasai twice a year – for a fortnight during the summer and then the Diwali vacations. We didn't really need a car. As a family, we didn't do outings and all. So then my parents decided to buy a secondhand scooter. Not a normal two-wheeler scooter though; this was one with a sidecar, so that all of us could travel together.

I loved sidecar scooters and was very excited with the thought of our family acquiring one. For weeks, I spoke of nothing else. When will our scooter come? What colour is it? Who will drive it? Where will we park it? Do I always have to sit in the sidecar? Can I sit behind

Baba sometimes? The parents answered good-naturedly. They were also looking forward to it.

But like every big thing which involved our family, it wasn't a smooth ride. Not at all. Once the news of us buying a scooter started circulating in the family, Tatya kaka (my dad's eldest brother) turned up, all agitated.

Tatya kaka (straight to the point): Chitra, is Abu (Baba was Abu to the rest of the family) buying a scooter?

Aai: Yes. We are getting a secondhand.

Tatya kaka: Have you lost your mind? Do you know how dangerous scooters are? The roads are full of traffic. That so-and-so kaku's son's skull was crushed under a truck just last month.

(Tatya kaka was what we called an extre-pessimist. He always took the most extreme position in the favour of caution. And he always had a gory story to prove his point. If you told him, "I am going to a circus", he would say, "There is no need. A tiger had run loose and attacked some people during a show some months back." Once, when I was staying over at their place, he had promised to take me and my cousins to Juhu beach. Then, after we were all ready to leave, about to wear our chappals, he cancelled the plan. All because I sneezed once. He promised to take us the next evening if I felt better. My cousins made me smother my sneezes and coughs in a pillow all evening so that we could have our outing the next day!)

Back to the scooter.

Aai: Yes. But we'll drive safely.

TK: Safe? Does that Abu even know the meaning of safe? He'll be a rash driver. I am sure.

Aai: No, Tatya. He will be careful.

TK: You guys don't even pray to God everyday. You don't even have a prayer space in your house! One hears of so many scooters toppling over these days.

Aai (a little relieved): Oh, this won't topple over. This has a sidecar for the kids.

TK: You mean you'll take Jaanu and Tanu also in that scooter? Don't you care for your children's safety?

Aai: Tatya, so many people drive scooters these days. They don't all topple.

TK: Let everyone do what they want. You don't have to follow them. Remember, that husband of yours is also hot-tempered. What if he hits someone? Do you know how the crowds beat vehicle-owners these days?

No one took that conversation seriously. Tatya kaka always assumed the worst. But Aai mentioned it to Baba nevertheless.

Aai: Tatya says it is dangerous to drive a scooter.

Baba (with long years of experience in defying his eldest brother): That Tatya is unnecessarily cautious. If he had his own way, the whole world would travel only in bullock carts.

Aai: But he said that you are a rash driver. That if you hit someone, the crowds will beat you up.

Baba: Don't listen to that Tatya. You know, he didn't allow Appa (Baba's sibling between him and Tatya) to drive back to Goregaon from Arnala after 5 p.m. He was scared that dacoits would attack the car. Dacoits! On the Mumbai highway from Vasai? Ha. They don't have any other business or what?

(I was on this trip to Arnala. And the dacoit warning sounded so hilarious, especially because Appa kaka was so law-abiding and God-fearing. He would have thrown his wallet before he was even asked. And he drove at 20 km/hr! At that rate, the dacoits could have looted us while the car was in motion.)

The only doubt we had was that Baba had not driven before. And considering that he was rather overconfident in other aspects of life, it was generally concluded that he would be a rash driver. So many in the family warned Baba to keep his cool while driving that it eventually made him lose it.

The scooter arrived after dinnertime one evening. It was a navy blue Bajaj scooter with a dainty sidecar next to it. There was a small expectant audience around: Baban kaka, the Nishigandha garage staff from across the street, the Shirsat kids, Akka and her half-dozen kids, who would anyway be playing on the streets at any time of the day. Aai did all the pooja; she put one tika on it, a small garland, offered the traditional diya, broke the coconut and all that.

Then some gully smartass suggested that the family go for a ride.

Baba: No. No. We'll go tomorrow.

Smartass: Arre, doctor, you should inaugurate it with your family.

Baba (laughingly): We have all the time in the world for that.

Me (with all my enthusiasm to show off to this small group): Yes, yes, Baba. Let's go for a ride now.

Aai: Yes, let's go.

Baba (relenting): Okay, let's go.

So my sister and I scrambled into the sidecar. My mum waited on the side for Baba to kickstart the scooter. And a small crowd of a dozen people waited expectantly for Doctor to take his family on a ride. I think it made my father very conscious. People who feel they know everything turn out to be very bad at doing things they don't know anything about.

Nervously, Baba started on the scooter and told my mum to sit behind him. Once the scooter sputtered to life, Baba rode it out of the compound. Our hearts lifted with happiness. Everything was fine – for exactly eight seconds. Just as Baba took a right and picked up speed to ride towards the Dadar Railway Quarters, Aai – with her infinite disbelief in Baba's efficiency – shrieked in fear.

Aai: Vasant. Go slow!

Baba (turning around and concentrating on his riding at the same time): Shut up. I'm going slow only.

Aai: Vasant (another shriek)! This is too fast. Too fast. Slow down. Slow down.

Now, the scooter wasn't going too fast. It was really not that big a deal. But I must have been seven at the time. Tanu must have been

two. Naturally, we also were alarmed by Aai's shriek and without understanding what was happening, we also started shouting.

Me: Baba. Baba. Stop the scooter.

Tanu: Baba. Stop. Baba. Stop.

Aai: Vasant, Vasant. Stop. You are going too fast.

Baba (again turning his head to look at Aai): Arre. Shut up, ch*^$#@! you all. Why are you screaming?

Me: Baba (wailing)

Tanu: Baba (wailing)

Aai: Vasant (wailing)

And wham! Baba ran straight into the electric pole 50 metres ahead, right outside Dhun Building. The jerky stop stilled our screams. We suddenly straightened up and looked around. The small crowd that had witnessed our takeoff and had started running towards us because of our screams had now slowed their gait. People in the Dhun and Cawrana buildings were now looking out of their windows. Baba rounded on us.

Baba: Bhe#&$&*d. Why were you screaming? See what happened.

Aai (sobbing): I told you to go slow. If you'd listened to me, we would not have bumped into the pole like that.

Baba: I bumped because you all started screaming. What were you shouting for?

Aai: You were going too fast.

Baba: I wasn't.

Aai: You...

By then the crowd had converged around us. Everyone was checking if we were alright. We were okay. Everyone had their comments.

"Thank God. Nothing happened. Sometimes scooters have such bad accidents."

"But what exactly happened, Doctor? You started off just fine."

"*Baap re*. The way Chitra was shouting, we thought your brakes were not working. You know, exactly like in films."

"No problem. Doctor will still take some time to learn."

"Somebody has put *nazar* (evil eye) on your new scooter."

Baba: Okay, okay. Now move back. I need to ride this thing back.

Aai: Be careful this time.

Baba: Shut up. (Then to no one in general) This woman will ruin me one day.

She didn't sit on the scooter. We still continued to sit dazed in the sidecar. Baba drove us back and parked the scooter. As is the case with anything that happens with my family, the versions varied drastically after this event.

Suppose someone asked, "How is your scooter?"

Aai: Arre, we had an accident that day. Vasant drove us straight into a pole.

Baba: It was not an accident. It was just a bump. And it happened because you were screaming.

Aai: Ha. Bump. It was a full-scale accident. You are too rash...

Baba: I am not rash. Do you know anything about driving? Does your father even know? Does he know anything other than train and BEST?

Aai: Ha ha. As if your father was born with a driving licence. Has anyone in Samant *khaandaan* ever owned a car?

Baba: Of course. My brother owns a car.

And so on and so forth. They never lived down that argument and they never forgave each other for it. Dad delivered a much better performance the next time we went out. Sometimes we went for a film to Plaza; sometimes we dared to drive to Goregaon on the first day of Diwali (we would arrive all dusty and grimy at Mothi kaki's home and had to wash up all over again after our Diwali bath). But it became clear pretty soon that Baba wasn't that much into driving.

For starters, he hated being in charge and then there was always this event hanging over his head. He started making excuses: "My hands/ back hurt from driving", "my eyes start itching", etc. The scooter was barely ridden. It got us into a lot of trouble over parking charges.

The society charged Rs. 40 a month for two-wheelers and Rs. 65 a month for four-wheelers. This scooter had three wheels, so the society charged us Rs. 65. But technically, it was a two-wheeler and my dad was adamant that he would pay only Rs. 40. Baba argued and argued. Sometimes through tough letters, sometimes with tough words. After we grew up a bit and stopped fitting into it, the sidecar was dumped to resolve the issue. Eventually, it just stood there, sturdy but forgotten. Aai got fed up and sold it off.

Yes, a vehicle is so much of a status symbol. But my parents never cared for any of it.

# 4.

# My Three Musketeers:

## Baban Kaka, Damu Kaka and Jagan Kaka

My parents weren't the only crackpots around me. There were quite a few specimens who could challenge a five-year-old's idea of normalcy in human behaviour.

The window on the left of our living room opened out to the ironing and laundry shop run by Baban Korgaonkar in our building's stilt parking. It was my window to the world outside. Baban kaka's shop had two wooden cupboards, where he stored ironed clothes. There was a large poster of Mithun Chakraborty in and as *Boxer* on one of those cupboards. There was a big table to keep bundles of clothes meant for ironing. People in the area would come with their clothes in one bundle and hang around much after Baban kaka had counted them all. They would talk of politics, films, cricket and all kinds of stuff with each other. It was a home base for all the servants in the locality.

*Istriwala* Baban kaka must have been my earliest friend and a rather unconventional solution to my mother's babysitting troubles. When I was an infant, Aai would leave me in a bundle with a milk bottle on his table when she had to rush out somewhere for a short while. When I was around three-four years old, she sacked my caretaker Dada and couldn't find a babysitter for a long time. At the time, since both of them worked, Aai-Baba would lock me inside our flat, keeping the window to Baban kaka's shop open, and go to work. My instructions were that I should always be in Baban kaka's line of vision. To do that, I had to stand on the sofa beside the window.

My lunch and water would be kept on the side so that I didn't have to go anywhere. Some of my earliest memories are from the hours I spent at this window, chatting with Baban kaka. It is the place where my love for trashy Hindi cinema began. I loved it.

When Baba left for work at 9.30 a.m., he would approach Baban kaka.

Baba: Baban kaka, keep an eye on her. (And to me) Jaanu, be a good girl. Don't trouble him.

Baban kaka: Don't worry.

Baba would leave. Then Baban kaka would start.

BK: So Jaanu, what do you want to do today?

Me: I'll sing something. *Nani teri morni?* (Baban kaka had taught me that song.)

BK: No, no. That's an old song.

Me: Twinkle, twinkle?

BK: Arre *dhat*. What are all these boring songs?

Me: Then what to sing?

BK: Chalo, I'll teach you a good song. You'll like it. Sing, '*Jaanu meri jaan*'.

Me: Hey, that's my name.

BK: Yes, isn't it a good song? Sing with me.

And we would sing the song together. There was '*Mamaiyya kero kero mama*', '*Yamma yamma*', '*Meri umar ke naujawaanon*', or '*Taaki re taaki*'. We had no TV at home then and Baban kaka was my sole connection to the film world.

BABAN ISTRIWALA
BOXER

Yes, Baban kaka was a big film buff and he is partly responsible for making me one too. He taught me Hindi. It was the *Ayela-Gayela Bambaiya* version of Hindi that Anthony Gonsalves spoke in *Amar Akbar Anthony.* It had words like *abbe, bundul* (not of good quality), *bakwaas, bheja, magaj, khali-pili, kayko, chal fut* and so on.

Every Friday evening he played hooky from his shop to watch a film. Every Monday morning, he'd tell me the story.

Me: Baban kaka, what film did you see on Friday?

BK: Arre, solid film it was. *Mawaali.*

Me: What does it mean?

BK: It means *badmaash*. But it has *mast* songs in it. (Singing) *Jhopdi mein charpai…*

Me: Wow. Tell me the story.

Baban kaka would then spend the next couple of hours telling me the story of *Mawaali*, all the while ironing and folding clothes and talking to the customers who dropped in.

Once he told me how Jaya Prada lifted Jeetendra in her arms in a song from the film *Haisiyat*. I was very impressed.

When Baba came home that afternoon, I asked:

Me: Baba, is Aai stronger than you or are you stronger?

Baba: I am stronger.

Me: Then can Aai lift you even though you are stronger?

Baba: No. Why do you ask?

Me: But Jaya Prada can lift Jeetendra. She's so strong.

Baba: Jaya Prada lifted Jeetendra? When?

Me: In a film.

Baba: Oh. In a film. Anything that happens in a film is all false.

Me: It is not. It is all real. She is very strong.

Baba: What rubbish. Who told you?

Me: Baban kaka said. He knows a lot about films.

Baba (rolling his eyes): Yes, sure.

Our living room window seemed to me like a television, this endless stream of people and Baban kaka's filmi storytelling seen through its frame.

Sometimes I would dance in that window, sometimes I would hang on that grill and try to scale it like a monkey. I would wear a dupatta and dance. And then I would imagine that I was on television, narrating the news, just like I had seen at my grandmum's house.

I would tell Baban kaka how I wanted to become a heroine. And he would tell me how people told him he looked like Ashok Kumar.

BK: You'll become a great heroine. You can dance well. But who will be your hero?

Me: Why do I need a hero?

BK: Every heroine needs a hero. There is no film without a hero.

Me: Who will become my hero?

BK: Hmm… don't worry. I'll become your hero.

Me: Sheee… You are so old.

BK: Even Ashok Kumar is old! Have you seen him when he was younger? He looked exactly like me. (Actually, he did.)

Me: No. Who is Ashok Kumar?

BK: You don't know Ashok Kumar? He was a bigger hero than your Sunny Deol, Mithun and Jackie Shroff.

I didn't even know any of these names then.

Me: Even bigger than Amita-Bachchan? (That's what I called Amitabh Bachchan)

BK: Of course. Okay, if you don't want me to be your hero, we'll have to find you another one. We'll ask Damu kaka.

Which brings me to Damu kaka. He was a regular at Baban kaka's shop. He was a short, portly man in his sixties who wore very thick glasses. Sometimes I would ask him to put his glasses on my nose. Everything would look foggy and I would feel giddy; I loved it.

Damu kaka was one of the last remaining employees of Chandubhai Shah's Ranjit Studio. By the time I was four or five, the studio had, along with the nearby Rooptara Studios, already started reeling towards extinction. Once upon a time, Damu kaka was a production assistant, working with big producers and stars, doing important things. Now he was just a dogsbody. He came to Baban kaka's shop to air his grouses and to play with me. He loved to outrage me.

BK: Damu, our Jaanu wants to become a heroine. Where do we find a hero?

DK: Who do you want?

Me (because I knew only one): Amita-Bachchan.

DK: He's too old for you. We'll get Jackie Shroff for you.

Me: Shee, who is Jackie Shroff? I don't want him.

DK: Don't act pricey like Meenakshi Seshadri. She also said she doesn't want Jackie and see where she is. Poonam Dhillon is doing all her films.

Me (petulantly): Okay.

DK: But there is a problem. Jackie Shroff loves to eat *khatmal* (bedbug) chutney with his meals.

Me: Sheeee... I don't want to work with him.

DK: Okay. Will Sanjay Dutt do?

Me: Okay, he will do. Is he very strong? Can he beat up ten men at one go?

DK: Yes but he is very danger in real life. He is cross-eyed and has a big stomach and one long tooth.

Me: What? Then how does he come on TV?

DK: That is because of the camera. Everyone looks good because of the camera only. You know your Hema Malini? She looks like a witch in real life.

Me: Really?

DK: Yes. I'd have asked Kumar Gaurav but he is too snobbish to be your hero. And he eats rats for breakfast.

Me: Shee… I don't want to become a heroine.

Damu kaka loved to rile me. Once he came during lunchtime and saw me eating a boiled egg in my window.

DK: So Jaanu, what are you eating?

Me: I am eating an egg.

DK: Whose egg?

Me: A hen's egg.

DK: *Hatt!* That doesn't look like a hen's egg to me. It is a duck's egg.

Me: No it is not. It is a hen's egg.

DK: How do you know? Have you ever seen a duck's egg?

Me: No.

DK: Okay, tell me, is its yolk yellow or grey?

Me: Grey.

DK: Exactly. Only the yolk of a duck's egg is grey.

Me: Nooooooo. Why will Aai give me a duck's egg?

DK: Because she also doesn't know. Tell me, has she ever eaten cockroach *usal?* How will she know?

That evening Aai would ask why I hadn't finished the egg.

Me: Shee. I don't want it. It is a duck's egg.

Aai (looking at me as if I've lost it): What? Duck's egg?

Me: Damu kaka was saying you gave me a duck's egg.

Aai: Stooppid. It was a hen's egg only.

Me: No. It was a duck's egg.

Aai: You think I don't know the difference?

Me: Have you ever eaten cockroach *usal?* How will you know how a duck's egg looks then?

Aai raised her eyebrows in exasperation.

Bedbug chutney, cockroach *usal*, baby lizard pulao, rat curry, cat *ka* mutton, goat's eye sandwich, ants and chapati, he did a swell job describing each in great gruesome detail. And I would listen with horror and fascination. He'd pick up an ant or a small cockroach and put it in his pocket, saying that he was saving it for dinner. When he was not talking about his gross culinary adventures, he would be busy planning my career as a film heroine.

DK: To be a heroine you have to have long hair. Like Rekha.

Me: I'll grow my hair. But they don't grow very long. (The truth was Aai didn't let me grow it at all. For years, she conned me by saying that cutting hair was the best way to grow it!)

DK: I can tell you how you can grow your hair faster. But you'll do 'shee...' again.

Me: No, no. Tell me.

DK: You have to boil some water, then put two green lizards in it, put some garam masala and ginger-garlic paste and drink it up slowly.

Me: Shee... Damu kaka. No.

DK: I told you. You are such a crybaby. (Then to Baban kaka) How will she become like Hema Malini if she doesn't have lizard soup?

BK: Then there is only one way. We'll have to kidnap a hero for her with the help of Jagan kaka.

Jagan kaka was my third friend. He was a gruff loner, who had lived in our gully much before any of us lived here. He came to Bombay to get a job with one of the cotton mills. But he didn't like the work and slowly, financial need and boredom pushed him to try out being a goonda. He liked being a goonda; he threatened and beat people for a living. He smuggled gold in the early days and then liquor during Emergency.

All I knew about goondas at the time was from the films, that they wore tight striped t-shirts, tight pants and for some strange reason, tied a handkerchief around their necks to look menacing. They also stood with their legs apart, warily juggling a knife in their hands.

Jagan kaka didn't look anything like that, except for the handkerchief around his neck. He was the gentlest, most affectionate person I knew. But he had ugly knife scars all over his body – one on his right breast, one that went from the back of his shoulder to his lower back and one on his thigh – and he liked boasting about the daring stunts he pulled.

BK: Jagan, we need to kidnap a hero.

JK: Why does she need a hero? All these heroes are *faaltu*.

Me: Huh? They can do so much fighting.

JK: Arre that's all *bandal* (fake) fighting. We are the ones who did the real fighting.

Me: You? How?

JK: Once three men stabbed me in the back and chased me all the way from Bhaucha Dhakka to Naigaon.

Me: Then what happened?

JK: I escaped. It's not easy to catch Jagan Sawant.

Me: But why did they attack you?

JK: Because I was a thorn in their way. They wanted to get rid of me.

Me: You didn't have a gun?

JK (scoffing): Real men don't need a gun. They fight with their bare hands.

The truth is that the revolver put Jagan kaka out of business. He was the king of the streets; he did *vasuli*, he bullied people, and like Don Corleone, he helped out people in tricky situations. Periodically, he was hired to bust textile mill strikes. He would threaten mill workers to make them go back to work. But he hadn't a clue about guns. According to him, when guns got into gang wars by the end of the '60s, real men got out of the business.

If you must kill, you must use your strength, he believed. Jagan kaka talked of *chaku* (knife) fights, being *tadipaar* (banished) and outrunning his rivals and the police. He once described how the police used to deal with goondas; they'd beat them sore and then screw around with the soles of their feet (smash some nerve here or there) so that they could never run very fast. True enough, Jagan kaka walked with a limp. I could have asked him to be my hero, true, but he didn't look very good. He wore a formal shirt and shorts, he couldn't dance and he sung quite terribly.

BK: You have very few choices. It's either me, Damu or Jagan.

Me: No. Jagan kaka is a goonda. He can only become the villain.

BK: Arre. Jagan is a big romantic. You don't know?

Me: Romantic means? You have a girlfriend, Jagan Kaka?

JK (bashfully): No, no. I'm not romantic. We'd make terrible heroes. We couldn't even be the heroes of our own films.

I learnt much later. At the height of his youth, Jagan Kaka had fallen in love with the street drunkard Mhadya's mute sister. But Jagan kaka's unconventional profession and caste came in the way and her vegetable-hawking parents of the Mali caste forbade them from marrying. Personally, I couldn't figure what their problem was. The girl was not extraordinary in any way, couldn't speak and was a complete shrew on top of that. She lived in the chawl right next to our building. Her bathroom window looked into our building compound.

She shuffled soundlessly in her house all the time, except when one of our *lagori* balls or shuttlecocks went into their house (their window panes were all broken and so the ball would go straight through). She would burst forth with some shrill, indecipherable noises in objection and make us run home in fear. The ball would be cut open and thrown back in our building compound after a few hours. If she had shown half that aggression for a week in objection to her parents, to be allowed to marry Jagan kaka, her grandchildren would have been playing with us.

Well, she didn't. The goonda didn't elope with the mute. He remained unmarried and she remained unmarried and they didn't even continue their love affair. This must have happened many years before I was born. By the time I was five or six, their only communication with each other would be infrequent and always through her window. Some nights, Jagan kaka would come drunk to Baban kaka's vacant table and sing lovelorn songs and she would shout some nonsense from her window.

The interaction went somewhat like this:

JK (in a way that would make it difficult to guess which song it was): *Pyar hua, ikraar hua...*

JK's girl (through her window at the top of her voice): *Kyaan kyaan kyaan kyaan...*

JK: Arre, who's telling you? Why don't you sleep? *Pyar hua...*

JK's girl (even louder): *Kyaan kyaan kyaan*

JK: *Chal jaa na...* don't eat my brain.

JK's girl (in a long volley): *Kyaan kyaan kyaan kyaan kyaan...*

JK: *Pyar hua... ikraar hua, pyar se phir kyu darta hai dil*

JK's girl (as if bursting a vessel): *Kyaan kyaan kyaan...*

Baba (popping his head out of our window): Oye, Jagan kaka, either you sing or let her sing. We can't handle both of you.

JK: Humpf (and walks off)

Sometimes he would defend the kids playing and request her to throw the ball back. But it resulted in the same manic shouting and Jagan kaka would again walk away sadly.

Baban kaka, Jagan kaka and Damu kaka were part of the legend of Loukik, intricately involved in the everyday running of our lives.

Over time, Jagan kaka, who lived in the shanty opposite ours, sold off his *kholi* (room) to garment manufacturer Haribhai. With a small bundle of clothes, he moved into Baban kaka's shop. He used to keep his clothes under the table. He would roam around the gully all day, doing odd jobs for people, and sleep on the ground in Baban kaka's shop at night. And every night he got drunk on country liquor and sang maudlin songs. His girlfriend objected, quite loudly. Then even that stopped; the girlfriend passed away and then the villain of the piece, her brother Mhadya, too passed away.

As I grew into my teens, Jagan kaka kept an eye on when and with whom I returned home. Sometimes he embarrassed me by pulling my cheek right on the street or slapping my back with his umbrella. By then the love songs had changed to patriotic songs and even those he sung badly.

Divya Bharati was the last big star to shoot at Ranjit Studio. That year, Damu kaka lost his job, his sense of humour and his fetish for insect kingdom recipes. His pants began to look more worn out and his specs were held together by strings. His married daughter lived nearby and took care of him. On most days, he would walk to Baban kaka's *dukaan* in a daze. If I said hi to him while going to school or college, he would look up abstractedly, suddenly remember me and ask, "Have you become a heroine?" I would laugh and reply, "No, Damu kaka. I can't have lizard soup." He would look at me like he didn't know what I was talking about and just raise a shivering hand to say bye. He passed away some years later.

Dada Kondke started making bilinguals and alongside the poster of *Boxer* and *Love 86* on Baban kaka's wooden cupboard in the shop, came the poster of *Andheri Raat Mein Diya Tere Haath Mein* and *Aage Ki Soch*. As time passed, Baban kaka too stopped watching films. He didn't have the stomach for Aamir Khan, Salman Khan or even middle-class love stories. "Your Aamir and Salman are not as stylish as Jeetendra. Their hair keeps falling over their faces, you know, like a dog," he would rue. Baban kaka retired in the mid-90s, some years after the Bombay riots.

But he comes every year for the Ganapati Utsav celebrations in our gully. He never fails to visit us. And every year, he tells my son about how my mother used to leave me with him when she had to rush to the grocer's. My son sang a song for him and Baban kaka remembered teaching me '*Naani teri morni*'. "He's just like you, Jaanu. You make him a hero now," he laughs.

Jagan kaka was right. These people were real heroes, entertaining and larger than life.

# 5.

# The Assassination of Indira and My New Dress

Another real hero of that generation was Indira Gandhi and one of the few days that pierced through the haze of my childhood was 31st October 1984. And I will tell you why I remember it so well – there was no TV transmission for 13 days because of this. The TV was only a few months old in our home at the time and the State mourning – we were subjected to Anup Jalota and Penaz Masani wearing white and singing mournful ghazals all day long – seemed too harsh to me at the time.

They dismissed school early that day. Just after the 1 p.m. lunch break, the class teacher came in and announced that we could go home. We just packed our books and rushed out, expecting her to take back her words any time.

A half-day out of the blue was indeed special. School was a bit of an *umar-qaid* (lifetime imprisonment) in those days. My parents used to be fussy about school attendance. High fever, loose motions, conjunctivitis, public bandhs and stone throwing, flooding, cold and cough – nothing deterred them from sending us to school. Even on days like Republic Day or Independence Day, when nothing was taught and we only had to stand in the sun or sit on the dusty ground, tolerating off-key reluctant songs of national pride or some minister-type fellow fumbling with the flag.

When we asked to bunk on such days, Aai would say with emphasis, "It is a day of pride for our country. Your great-grandparents have fought for our freedom. Only selfish people would bunk school on such a day."

[To be honest, my great-grandfather, S. K. Patil, was indeed a freedom fighter. He eventually became a mayor and then a Union minister. My dad's family also had its share of freedom fighters. Two of my father's mamas (maternal uncles) in Virar also had a freedom fighter certificate framed on their walls but Baba insisted they were bogus. Apparently, it was just the day after Gandhiji announced the salt satyagraha. My dad's disreputable maternal uncle, Antu mama, had kept a container with some *mandeli* (small fish) and sea water out in the sun while he went across the street to buy beedi. The local police thought that he was trying to make salt with it and arrested him and his brother Shankar. It is said that Antu mama and Shankar mama returned from jail after a short while, having pinched the rugs and aluminium tumblers from there. One of the rugs was given as a Raksha Bandhan gift to one of their sisters as well. The family swore on the quality of those rugs, it seems.]

Anyway, on days like Bombay Bandh, heavy rains and flooding, when other parents worried for the safety of their children and preferred that they stay at home, mine worried about our school attendance.

Me: Baba, I don't want to go to school tomorrow.

Baba: No, you must go.

Me: Arre, it is Bombay Bandh. There will be stone-throwing. It is dangerous.

Baba: Nothing will happen.

Me: But they will anyway send us back early then.

Baba: Yes, so then come back when they tell you that. But you must go to school.

Being sent home without being asked to was indeed a miracle. I was in the third standard. Shalaka (Pinky), my friend from the building, and I always walked home together. She was a cute, plump girl. I was extremely scrawny (people called me a single *pasli*) and gully folks called us *Jaadya-Radya* (Marathi name for Laurel and Hardy.)

On most days, the two of us took our time coming back; the street would be busy and we would sing Hindi film songs or tell each other make-believe stories. Sometimes we wore our chappals like gloves on our hands, or closed our eyes and walked; sometimes we walked backwards. It was common to bump into people while one did this. Not on that day. It was quiet on the street when we were returning. Quiet streets only happened at the time of a cricket match or the film telecast on Sunday evening and in later years, *Ramayan*.

When we reached home:

Baba: How come you are back from school?

Me (quickly moving to change my clothes): Yes, something happened. They sent us back. What happened? How come they sent us back?

Baba: Someone has assassinated Indira Gandhi.

Even at that age, I knew Indira Gandhi was an important person. I was aware that my parents were critical of her politics. But I was also aware that they were proud that she was India's first woman prime minister.

Once when I complained tearfully to Baba:

Me: Baba, Aai forcibly cut my hair.

Baba: So what's wrong? You look beautiful.

Me: I don't. I want long hair. Girls don't have boy cuts.

Baba: Indira Gandhi does. And she is such a smart woman. You must become like her one day.

That was his way of comforting me. He used to say, "Look at Indira Gandhi. Look at how intelligent she is. You must become independent like her." Indira was a role model for my family.

To come back to the point, I also wanted to know the meaning of assassination.

Me: What is assissi..?

Baba: Assassinated. When a political person is murdered, it's called assassination.

Me: Who murdered Indira Gandhi?

Baba: One of her guards shot her with a rifle.

Me: But why?

Baba (shook his head): Because of politics.

Me: Oh. Can I go and play?

Baba (sigh): Yes.

So happily I went out and announced to all my building friends that Gabbar Singh had killed Indira Gandhi.

It was my first lesson in religion I think. I was aware about the Sikhs. Not because of Sardar jokes but because of Balbir who lived in the shanty right across from our house. He was a few years older than me and had long hair which he washed every Sunday on the footpath outside his house. I knew, therefore, that Sikh men grew their hair and tied it up in a turban and their wives wore loose salwars on very tight kameezes and didn't wear bindis. To me, the world's religions at the time were divided into two groups: those in which women wore bindis and those in which women did not wear bindis.

I was also somewhat aware in theory that people of my religion disliked people of other religions and vice versa. I was told by my parents that such people were stupid.

The locality around Loukik had a dense secular fabric. We were exposed to the neighbourhood Javedbhai, who ran a bicycle rental shop, and then Ijazbhai and Yunusbhai, the truck mechanics at the Nishigandha garage. Along with the other Hindu teens who whiled away time at the street junction, these boys would also tease me, singing '*Tu mera jaanu hai, tu mera dilbar hai*' loudly whenever I passed by them. (My family and the rest of the gully folks called me Jaanu, short for Janhavi. And that song from Subhash Ghai's *Hero* briefly made my life miserable. I hated the song.)

I must have been six and usually accompanied by my dad, who would chuckle when I scowled at these boys. Then when I became angry and told off my dad for not scolding them or turned my head away, one of them would approach with a chocolate to pacify me. Sometimes, because they knew I hated it, these garage boys would put grease on my cheek. They wore grease-worn overalls throughout the year, but on Eid they wore shiny white clothes with gold chains.

Balbir was part of this group of boys, none of whom were to be seen on this particular evening.

There was quiet and unease in Bombay that evening. The only other times I have noticed that kind of silence in the city was much later during the Babri Masjid riots and then the bomb blasts. This was the first time.

There was disquiet at home too. My parents were heatedly discussing conspiracy theories about Khalistan and the Sikhs. My parents wanted to know what was really happening. But the radio hadn't announced her death yet. There was fear for the Sikhs in the North. Over the next two-three days, Baba would ask Balbir's dad about how things were with his family in Delhi. And everyday Balbir's dad would sadly shake his head. People were discussing the murder everywhere: at the dinner table, barber's shops, the grocers'.

(Mhangrya, our rude, garrulous and openly abusive fisherman came a couple of days later, to offer a fresh batch of pomfret. Baba wasn't home to check it out. Offended, he asked, "Has your *baapu* gone for Indira's funeral now?")

I also experienced disquiet. But I had a bigger reason for gloom than fear for the future of Congress. It was my mum's younger brother Vishwas mama's wedding on November 8. I wondered miserably if Indira Gandhi's death would make my grandfather cancel the wedding.

Weddings weren't a haldi-mehendi-sangeet-pheras-reception magnum opus in those days, at least not Maharashtrian weddings. Maharashtrians didn't have any dance or sangeet before the wedding night or anything; there would just be an endless queue of women

NATION MOURNS
PM INDIRA GANDHI'S
DEATH

bending and stashing rice grains and coconuts in the bride's lap. If we could, the youngsters in the family would meet up and mix mehendi powder in water and draw it on our own hands with matchsticks. I can tell you, we did some pretty bizarre designs at the time.

My mum, her sisters and cousins bleached each other's faces and shaped each other's eyebrows with a thread. (In one of these said weddings, my mum applied bleach to her eyebrows in a quest to shape them like Rekha's and ended up looking like, in Baba's words, Captain Spock!)

To come back to Vishwas mama's wedding, the ceremony itself used to be boring. Ustad Bismillah Khan would be whining in the background, with a *pangat* style lunch where *varan bhaat* (dal chawal) and vegetables, *usal* (pulses) and dahi were served to a long line of seated guests. No chappal stealing or multi-cuisine buffets with special tawa items and chaat or Chinese counters or anything. And at the reception, there actually would be no dinner. It was the trend to be served ice cream, just a slab of plain vanilla. And my grandmother would make eyes at us on our second helping and whack us on the third.

As kids, it didn't matter much. We would anyway just frantically run round and round and round the wedding hall, till we were herded together to have lunch or till we fell right on our faces or till one of us either lost a chappal, hairpin, or worse, a gold earring or ring.

My mama's wedding was a high point for our family. My mum had ordered a pretty pink dress for me to wear at the wedding. It was light pink with shiny blue dots on it. The design I had chosen had a small collar and a big flounced skirt. My grandmother had bought me the dress material from the US and my mum had waited for a big enough occasion to stitch it. For most weddings, girls in our family would be given a *parkar-polka* to wear. A *parkar polka* is a Maharashtrian version of the ghagra-choli without a dupatta, except that it was always made of someone's old silk or *kanjivaram* saree and extremely hazardous to human life.

The problem was that the women in my family always tried to yield two-three small outfits from the same saree. This meant that the economised girth of such a *parkar* (skirt) would be so constricted that one couldn't stretch one's legs wider than 9 inches or take big strides without tripping hard on the face. Sometimes the saree border would start coming off and trip us while running anyway.

The advantage of this outfit was that one couldn't get lost in the wedding crowd; people would recognise the family you were from based on the outfit's material.

But mama's wedding was special. I would be wearing a pink frock. With the Indira Gandhi crisis and all those Indira fans in our household, my big fear was that the marriage would get cancelled or postponed. It was a crushing, sad sort of worry: who thinks about frivolous material things like a dress when our nation was in such a crisis? Something similar to what baby Indira must have felt before throwing her foreign doll in the fire when Gandhiji gave the call to go Swadeshi.

So a few days later, I sat moping at the dinner table, playing with my food. In the middle of narrating how people actually cried the day Pandit Nehru died, my mother noticed:

Aai: Jaanu, why aren't you eating your food? Do you want anything?

Me (in a small voice): No.

Aai: Then what's wrong? Why are you looking so sad?

Me: Aai, what will happen to Vishwas mama's wedding?

Aai: What will happen means? It is on 8th.

Me: But now that Indira Gandhi is dead…

Aai: What does that have to do with it?

Me (perking up): It is not cancelled?

Aai: No. Why should we cancel it?

Me (a little happily now): Oh. And my dress? The tailor will give my dress in time for it, na?

Aai (with a smile): So that's what you are worrying about? If the tailor doesn't stitch it on time, we'll have to buy you a readymade one for the ceremony. Chalo, now don't make such a mournful face. Eat fast.

Incidentally, my tailor could not really deliver my dress, even by the morning of the wedding. So my mum did have to go and buy a readymade dress for me at the last minute. That dress was Poonam Dhillon style – blue with a white dotted flap at the front, short sleeves, and a tight skirt. My mum put lipstick on my lips and warned me that it would rub off if I talked too much. I must have kept my mouth shut for exactly eight minutes. The tailor delivered my pink dress in the afternoon of the wedding, right in time for the evening reception, where in all my delight, I ate three plates of vanilla ice cream. And that is my memory of Indira Gandhi's death.

# 6.

# Nazia Enters Our Life

Then, around 35 years ago, in September 1985, an international sample called Nazia arrived at 1, Loukik and irrevocably changed the way its residents and its neighbours lived, spoke and loved.

It had been a difficult patch. My sister was a toddler and our live-in babysitter and help of five months, Sugandha, had been asked to return home that summer. Unfortunately, my mother hadn't been able to find a créche or nanny for us. Vacations were always worse without babysitting support. We experienced several babysitters in those five months. Mind you, my mother wasn't fussy. (As mentioned earlier, my earlier babysitter had been a man called Dada, who played *matka* at the local centre.)

One babysitter came for a day, stole my mother's chappals and ran away. Another was an old homeless woman, who insisted she could handle the work and then after a day's work, fell ill for two days. But even after sending my sister off to my grandmother's and adjusting my dad's and her own schedules in some convoluted way, my mother had to lock me up in the house for many hours a day. She wasn't particularly happy with it.

Then suddenly one evening, a male colleague of my mother's, whom she had never before spoken to in office, brought home Nazia. He had overheard Aai wailing about needing live-in help to someone else in office and brought it upon himself to find someone for her.

The girl, he said, would live with us, work for us and did not expect to be paid very much as long as my mother fed her and clothed her and would immediately start working with us. My mother couldn't believe her luck. She still can't believe it. "God knows where we found you," she says in exasperation to Nazia to date.

Thirty-five years ago, Nazia was a thin, squiggly girl with angry eyes and a prickly attitude. I was eight. She wore a worn-out polyester grey salwar kameez and sat on the floor, clutching her small *potli* of clothes and possessions. Her hair was long, jet black and silky and she smelt funny.

She kept looking at our floor tiles with great concentration. She didn't know how to cook or clean or run a house but she'd learn, the man said and left without telling us whom to call if things didn't work out.

As soon as he left, I sat across her on the floor and stared. After tolerating it for 20 seconds, Nazi flashed her angry eyes at me.

N: What are you looking at? Am I naked or something?

I did a double take. Nobody in the world had talked to me like that. I shook my head.

Me: What is your name?

N: Nazia.

Me: What is your full name?

N: I don't know.

Me: Where have you come from?

N: I don't know. You are going to tell me to leave if I don't tell you?

I widened my eyes and left. I told Aai.

Me: Where has she come from?

Aai: Nagpur.

Me: Why doesn't she talk properly?

Aai: It's okay. She must be feeling awkward. Let her be. She'll be okay after a while.

The next day after my mother left for work, Nazia did all the work she was supposed to but didn't touch anything else. She didn't have a bath because Aai hadn't specifically told her she could use the bathroom or the soap or the oil. She also snubbed all my attempts at idle conversation while we were left with each other.

Me: You smell funny. You haven't had a bath?

N: No. Your mother hasn't said that I could use the bathroom.

Me: Arre, you can use the bathroom.

N: Your mother hasn't said so.

Me: But she won't mind.

N: I don't use anything I am not meant to.

Silence.

Me: Where do your parents live?

N: *Jahannum.*

Me: Where is that?

N: Nowhere.

Me: How did your hair grow so long?

N: Like that only.

Me: I also want long hair like yours but Aai doesn't let me grow it.

N: Hmm.

Me: When I grow up, I want my hair to be long enough to reach my calves.

N: Hmm. How much you talk. Can't you keep quiet?

Silence. Her whole persona was strange.

It was really mysterious behaviour for a live-in help. As job descriptions go, girls who qualify for live-in help have to have:

- A certain sway in their walk

- An unbecoming fringe like Poonam Dhillon or Sadhana over their foreheads

- A habit to spend really long hours in the window looking at people in the street

- An unnaturally loud giggle

- Strange admirers and hangers-on, wearing exceptionally tight pants, who follow them around on the street and in the garden, talking surreptitiously and treating the children in their care to candy and chocolates

Nazia spoke respectfully in monosyllables to Aai-Baba but snapped at me and Tanu. When she didn't work around the house, she sat defensively in one corner and stared at the tiles. She didn't speak to anyone outside the house and most of all, because we slept with her in the same room, she refused to let us switch on the fan because it made her feel cold!

Over a couple of days, she became a little less prickly. She also had a bath after I told my mother.

Aai: Nazi, haven't you had a bath?

N: No. You didn't say I could use the bathroom.

Aai: Of course, you can use the bathroom and anything in it.

N: Ok. I will have one tomorrow.

Aai: No. Go right now.

N: No. I will go tomorrow.

The next day when she opened her *potli* to take out her stuff for the bath, I peeked in from behind her. I had been very curious about her small bag.

Me: What is in your *potli?*

N: Why do you want to know?

Me: Just like that.

N: You can see after I come from my bath.

I waited patiently; she came out of the bath in a green polyester dress, dried her long hair with her dupatta and then opened her *potli*. There was a half comb, a black string, a red ribbon, small Ponds cans with talcum powder in them, and another tin box of Ponds Dreamflower talc, in which she kept a couple of bangles, a pair of earrings, a nose ring and a kajal box. She showed it to me and then kept it all back in the drawer that she had been allotted.

Nazia's softening towards my family was very slow and complex. The biggest barrier was her language. She spoke Hindi and to my family, people only spoke Hindi in films. My mother thought adding *–oonga* to anything Marathi made it Hindi. And since she only spoke to *bhajiwala bhaiyyas*, it worked.

"*Yeh watana kaisa denga?*" (How much are these peas for?)

"*Arre tum khup mahag deta hai.*" (Oh, you are charging a very high price.)

With Nazia, it turned pretty comical.

"*Dekho, khane ke baad yeh ota dhoneka.*" (See, wash the kitchen platform after you eat.)

Since Nazia didn't know that an *ota* meant kitchen platform in Marathi, she didn't know what exactly to do.

"*Arre sharmati kayko? Sharmane ka nahi. Bindast rehne ka idhar.*" (Why are you feeling shy? Don't be. Relax.)

Since Nazia didn't know what *bindast* meant, she let that go.

"*Wo bhanda use mat karo; usme karap jayenga.*" (Don't use that utensil; it will burn.)

Nazia would look quizzically since she didn't know the meaning of *bhanda* (utensil), the English word 'use', as well as *karap* (burn).

She didn't know why my mother said "*Aa rahi hu*" (I am coming) when she was actually going. And she didn't know why my mother couldn't get her Deccani *hau* (yes) and *nakko* (no) and *uno* (them there) and *ino* (them here). We didn't know the meaning of *sabar karo* (have patience) or *bhooknike* (blasted) or *ikka-dukka* (one or two). We didn't know *batata* was called *aloo* and *kanda* was called *pyaaz*.

For quite a while, it appeared futile. Nazia was stilted as it is and the interaction through demonstration wasn't working. My sister and I had already given up, wondering if the impatient Nazia would ever stick around. But slowly Aai and Nazia came to terms with each other and would you believe it, the breaking point was hair oil.

Once Aai complained of hairfall.

Aai: Tch. How much my hair is falling.

Then out of the blue, without ever having once gotten into a conversation without being asked, Nazia spoke.

N: Have you tried methi oil?

Aai: No. How to make it?

N: I'll make it tomorrow.

That night she soaked methi in water, then fried some curry leaves or something in coconut oil and mixed the methi and so on. That evening, she gave my mother the oil. My mother was quite thrilled and applied some on everybody's heads, sure that methi was the thing. The rest of the oil was kept on the kitchen platform.

The next day we all woke up to a funny smell.

Baba: *Saala*, what is this smell? Chitra, have you kept some food out?

Aai: No. But yes, something is smelling. Jaanu, check if some rat has died outside.

They checked everything in the fridge. I checked outside. Nothing.

Baba: Yuck, it is smelling like… like… rotten fish.

Aai: You Samants always think of fish only.

Baba: Has anyone in your *khaandaan* ever eaten fish? This is what it smells like after it has rotten.

Aai: Ha, only your *khaandaan* is a PhD in fish matters. We all have grown up on the streets na. Check under the sink if the drain pipe has choked. The smell is coming from there.

Baba: Nothing under the sink. Pipe is okay. Check the grain *dabbas*.

Aai: No it's all dry there.

Baba: Then what could it be? (Looking around, spotting the hair oil container) What is in that?

Aai: Hair oil that Nazia prepared.

Baba (checking it and deeming it the culprit): It is coming from here. What is this rubbish?

Aai: It cannot be that. That is hair oil.

Baba: Here, smell it. It smells like a dead rat. Throw it.

Aai: No. No. It is a herbal oil; it's not so bad.

Baba: Are you mad? Your baap has made hair oil like this? The whole house is stinking.

Aai: It's not stinking so much. Nazia has made it. I'll bottle it.

She bottled it, innocent in her belief that it was really her answer to hairfall. But really, by the next day, the smell was unbearable. And Nazia, for the first time, spoke to Aai on her own initiative.

N: Didi, *bahut baas aa rahi hai* (it's stinking a lot). Throw that oil. I'll make it fresh for you. It's smelling like, like...

Me: Shee-shee? (And Nazia laughed softly, pursing her lips together in an embarrassed sort of way.)

Aai, stumped at Nazia's laugh, just nodded. The hair oil was dumped in the plants. Slowly, awkwardly, Aai became Didi and Nazia became Nazi, and true to her name, she took complete control of the household. She decided what grains to buy, what pulses to soak to be cooked the next day, what brush to buy to clean the toilet, how to fold the clothes, when I should start studying and also whether I studied or not.

When my mother was not there, the illiterate Nazi would scold me for loitering around.

N: Shouldn't you be studying? Where are your books?

Me: Okay.

Taking out a story book wouldn't help.

N: This is not your school book. This is a story book.

Me: How do you know if you can't read it?

N: There are pictures on this book's cover. Open a school book.

Impeccable logic. So I randomly took out study books and dawdled around.

N: Why aren't you studying?

Me: I am. See these books?

N: How can I tell you are studying? Read loudly.

Me: Arre I'm writing. How can I do that loudly?

N: Read out aloud whatever you are writing. Else you will become like me, *gawaar*, having to do housework.

Phew. To convince Nazi, my sister and I really had to study aloud like that right until college. We read everything out aloud. Till my MCom finals, Nazi would abruptly call out from the other room.

N: Jaanu, have you slept off?

Me: No. Why?

N: I can't hear you read. Why aren't you studying?

Me: Just reading up something. Go to sleep.

N: Yes. But I'm keeping a watch!

She decided how many rotis I should eat and how much water I should drink. She decided which friends of mine I should continue with and which I should dump.

N: That Megha, Poonam are no good. You shouldn't be playing with them.

Me: Why?

N: They have flunked twice so far. Do you want to be like them?

Me: Why will I be like them?

N: Because you spend time with them. You should spend time with people more intelligent than you.

Me: How would you know that they are not intelligent? You don't know how to read or write yourself.

N: They can't speak one line properly in English. They are no good.

It may have taken Nazia a year or so to warm up to us; we don't even know when it happened. We don't know whether it was when she first told us the '*Ek rupaye mein doodhi halwa*' story or whether it was when she first taught us how to build a *zopdi* or tie a *burkha*.

Maybe it was when she first made fried chicken or when we nursed her through her TB convalescence. We don't know when she stopped pushing us away when we kissed or hugged her spontaneously and when she started pecking or hugging us herself. We don't remember when she first agreed to sleep with the fan on. But we took it for granted. Slowly we learned to accept her moody warmth and ignore her weird prickliness.

For instance, the first time I lost a pen.

Me: Aai, have you seen my new pen?

Aai: Why don't you keep it carefully? I am not buying you a new one. Ask Nazi if she's seen it.

Me: Nazi, have you seen my new pen?

N: What do you mean? Do you think I have taken it?

Me: Of course not. But...

N: You think I would steal a pen? Are you accusing me?

Me: No. No. No.

N: I have never touched a thing that is not mine. I have always lived an honest life. (Eyes filling with tears) This is what happens when you live in someone else's house. You have to live on their terms. Nobody trusts you. It is better I leave this house only.

Me: Huh? I just asked if you have seen the pen.

Aai (in a soft tone): She is not accusing you. She was only asking if you've seen it. Nobody is accusing you.

N (sniffing): Ha. If she were not accusing, why would she ask? I'll leave this house only.

She started moving around the house in agitation. But strangely, when we expected her to pack and leave, she abruptly came and plonked my pen on the book I was reading.

N: Do not ever accuse me of stealing. I am not a *chor*.

By this time, even I was in tears.

Me: But I never did. I just asked… Nazi, are you going to leave us? I didn't say you took it. Please don't go.

N: Why should I leave? I have done nothing wrong.

And calmly she would return to whatever she was doing.

The next time I asked her if she'd seen my bag, the same episode occurred. It's been over 30 years now; she still threatens to leave. Once at the end of a similar episode Baba wondered aloud, "Where has this sample come from?"

The truth is, we don't really know. Truly.

# 7.

# Where Could Nazia Have Come From?

Yes, it is possible. Nazi has cohabited with us for 35 years and we still have no clue where she has come from, who her family is, why she chose to leave and disown them and why she decided to own us. Hundreds of people have asked and wondered from where we got such a lovely house help, how old she is, and how in the world have we managed to convince her to slave away at our home for three decades. But the woman herself is tight-lipped.

At first, we were so surprised and gratified with her joining our family that we never bothered to press her about it. And later, it simply did not matter.

In all these years, she has never once revealed a single coherent story about her own past, apart from a few bits and pieces about her growing up, but the stories are so inconsistent that they are impossible to string together.

The biggest inconsistency is Nazi's real age. She doesn't know when she was born and what major events may have occurred around her age. She only knows that she was born near the New Year, but whether that was the Hindu, Gregorian or the Islamic calendar, God only knows. When she came to our house, she was definitely older than a teenager, at least above 17. Then, 35 years at our place makes her 50 years old. But the problem is Nazi looks barely a day older than 35.

Nazi, of course, doesn't help at all. She keeps changing her life stories so much that none of it makes any sense.

So here are some of the stories she's narrated to us:

1. Nazi's mum and dad had a love marriage. Her mum was a North Indian Muslim and her dad was a South Indian from Madras. How did they come to Nagpur she has no idea. Her father traveled a lot to sell sarees. His mother (Nazi's dadi) was extremely strict, a *burkhewali* and never accepted either her non-burkha wearing daughter-in-law or any of her grandchildren. There were in all five children (Salim, Arif, Asif, Anjum and Nazia, who was the youngest). However, the names of her siblings kept changing. I suspect the only person she was fond of was her sister and Asif. But nobody knows what happened to them and Nazi has never kept in touch with any of her family since she entered our lives. Nazi's mother died and her father married again and the stepmother drove the kids to the street. (This may have some truth, going by her tearful response to my enthusiastic narration of Hansel and Gretel to my son!) They had to steal sometimes to eat. Nazi also talked about how she was taken to a remand home because she stole some oranges.
2. There is another story which could also be true, except that it is not consistent with the first one. While describing how she got that big cut across the parting of her hair, she explained that her mum baked and sold biscuits and cookies at Chandrapur station and once threw a sharp baking utensil at her in anger. Their father deserted her and later Nazi's mum became insane and had to be institutionalised. And that drove the kids to the streets.

3. Then while narrating the story of a haunted haveli in Nagpur near her dadi's house, she talked of how strict and organised her dadi was. She had a full head of white hair, made soft idlis and lovingly fed her grandchildren.

4. Nazia was supposed to have come to Mumbai with her brother (so said the man who brought her to us). Nazi says the brother

was a cook with Taj. She'd been living in his *kholi* before she came to our place. But that brother has never ever bothered to inquire about her (unless Nazi has been calling him secretly, but somehow I don't believe that. And I am too scared of asking her if she is). And whenever we have asked why he has never called her or why she has never called him, she scoffs and says, "*Woh saala haraami.* Why should I call him?"

5. In the middle of all this, she talked about working in Nagpur at the home of a doctor called Salim, whose wife was really sweet, took care of Nazi and gave her her old dresses. However, when asked why she left them to come to Mumbai, she has no answers.

6. She talks about how she loves watching films, especially ones starring Amitabh Bachchan, back to back in theatres. She really must have, because she knew about all the films we saw on video. But you ask her how she found the money to watch films in theatres, she retorts, "What? You think only rich kids like you can watch films in theatres? Poor kids can't?"

7. She claims she doesn't know how to read and write. She's screwed up phone messages and numbers countless times. She can't count. Yet, she knew exactly when I started bluffing about my studies. She knew exactly when I would be bunking classes and going for a film in college. She understands English clearly; even difficult terms like 'comprehend' or 'complicated' or 'loser'.

Because of these inconsistencies and my inherent flair for filmi drama and intrigue, I have come up with a few theories about Nazia too. You could be forgiven for thinking that they are outrageously filmi.

1. The biggest suspicion is that Nazi could be a Pakistani spy or terrorist. She may have come into the country during the war and, pained by the destruction and violence she saw, she decided to reform and work as a house help! At our house!

2. Fed up with an alcoholic father, an insane mother and persistent poverty, she may have run away from home, found a benefactor in the man from Aai's office (who she never mentions or remembers, by the way) and found her way to our house.

3. Sometimes, observing her complete prudishness and prickliness at being touched and her extra cautiousness with us, she may have been a victim of abuse. Her parents may have tried to sell her off to a pimp and she may have run away from a brothel. Of course, Nazi rejects this theory vehemently.

4. More outrageously, she could be the abandoned illegitimate daughter born to my own mother before marriage who had returned to search for her mother. Aai rejects this theory vehemently.

5. She may have run away from home to get married and found that the man was a, in her own words, *haraami* and so left him to look for a job.

Marriage is a touchy subject. According to Nazi, this world is full of *haraamis* and she doesn't want to get married. All our family and friends who understand our love for her, wonder why she hasn't married yet. Well, it isn't much of a mystery.

Being a Muslim girl in a Hindu world, Nazi couldn't find any proposals from good boys in our community as well.

Although one or two elderly relatives, like my mother's chachi and her sister, stopped eating or drinking water at our place after Nazi arrived, her Muslimness was never a problem with us. In fact, Nazi's biryani was a big hit in the family and her recipe is now practised globally in all our cousins' households.

Other than the fact that Nazi could count till three in Arabic and followed the alphabet right to left, there was no way anyone could have identified her as a Muslim. Very soon, after starting to live with us, Nazia had started dressing like my mother – sober cotton clothes, flat sandals and a bindi on her forehead – while we took on some of her habits – wearing kajal, salwar kameezes and eating biryani and *sheer khurma*.

It was only during the height of the '93 Babri Masjid riots when our well-meaning society members came to request us to ask Nazi to leave, because it could mean danger for all the society members, that we realised Nazi's 'otherness'.

I remember my father getting so upset that he threw all of these well-meaning society members out of the house, shouting, "Nazi will stay with our family, her family. Let them kill all of us together." He shouted it so loudly in the doorway by the street that we were afraid someone would actually hear and start getting ideas to slaughter us.

But, in our few attempts to find a boy for Nazi, we realised that secularism doesn't find many real-life practitioners. The mystery around her age and her illiteracy was another handicap. But the biggest factor for Nazi's single state is her own incredible snobbishness.

Once Bharti kaki excitedly called my mother. She knew a good Muslim boy in Vasai who would have been suitable for Nazi. She asked Aai to talk to Nazi about it.

Aai: Nazi, are you interested in getting married?

N: No. Why? You have someone interesting for me?

Aai: Yes. He lives in Vasai.

N (with a lot of mistrust): What does he do?

Aai: He has a *kanda-batata* (onions and potatoes) cart.

N: Shee. I don't want to marry an *aloo-pyaaz* wala.

Aai: Then what? You want a doctor?

N: Why not? At least some decent service. I come from an educated, respectable family.

Aai: Ha. Which?

N: You are not educated and respectable or what?

And that shut my mother up. Then next, someone else, aware of Nazi's demand for a businessman, suggested a rickshaw-wala with his own *kholi* .

Aai: Nazi, there is another boy for you.

N (sceptically): Sure. What does he do?

Aai: He runs a rickshaw. He is well-to-do. He even has his own *kholi*.

N: Shee. *Kholi?* Means?

Aai: He has his own room in a chawl.

N: Shee. Chawl! I don't want to live in a chawl. Where do you find such *faaltu* boys?

Aai: *Faaltu*! He is earning Rs. 5,000-6,000 a month!

N: Yes, but he lives in a chawl. Who will live in a chawl? You know how hard I have worked to come from the streets to live in a clean, decent home? You want me to go back to the street again? Would you look for a boy like that for your own daughter?

Nazi's favourite argument tactic has always been to attack Aai's sense of fairness in dealing with her as her own daughter. Solid guilt trip. It always shuts Aai up.

Aai: No. But who will marry an illiterate girl?

N: Why? Illiterate girls are not human? They don't have a right to live?

Aai (pacifying): No. No. That's not....

N: Then? I'm a burden to you? You want me to leave the house? I am not your own daughter na? I'm somebody else's. (Again, with eyes tearing up) Come Nazi, it's time to find a home for yourself.

There is no need for all this drama. But the truth is, this threat has been working in Nazi's favour for all these years. She uses it routinely to get us to eat our medicines, drink milk everyday, study, and a hundred other things. And no matter what the original subject is, she comes right down to this point.

For instance, if the rice is a little overcooked or if the food has too much salt.

Baba: Who's put the salt in the dal?

N (checking): Just a little salty.

Baba (in a teasing tone): Little? Have you put *namak* in the dal or dal in the *namak*?

N (tears welling up in her eyes): It's just a little *namak*. (Then muttering) This is what happens when you live in somebody else's house. They treat you like a slave. They think they own you.

Baba: What does that have to do with the *namak* in the dal?

N: It is better to leave only. Why should I live here where there is no *izzat*?

Baba sighs. Eats dinner quietly. End of matter.

Then when Baba would return tired from the dispensary, she would bring a cup of chai to him.

Baba (gratefully): Thanks Nazi. Just what I needed.

N: Then what? Would your own flesh-and-blood do this for you?

Baba sighs. Sips chai quietly.

Many conflicts in our house have been resolved in this easy, fluid manner. Over the years, the family too has gotten used to her quicksilver moods; the deep love with which she holds us together, makes us her own and then the quick, prickly way in which she disowns us and makes us her mere employers.

To be honest, it can't have been easy living with our mad family. Nazi brought order to our chaotic household. We were a family where school uniforms were given for ironing five minutes after emerging from the bathroom on a Monday morning.

After Nazi came, we became a family where uniforms were ironed and ready on Saturday evening. We took roti, ghee and sugar in our tiffins because my parents were too busy to go vegetable shopping. We became a family where tiffins began to be planned in advance.

The *raddi* started getting sold on time; groceries were ordered in on the first Saturday of every month. We realised the comfort of order in planning. Nazi continues to live with my mum at 1, Loukik.

As I write this, she is pottering around in my kitchen, making parathas for me, muttering about the way I run my house.

Me: While you are at it, can I get a chai?

N: Hmm. Stop working in front of the computer for these long hours.

Me: Arre do I sit everyday? I am just caught up in finishing this. I am writing about you only.

N: Ha. What? I am some film star or what?

In five minutes, she plonks a cup in front of me. It is *nariyal paani.*

Me: Where's the chai? I want chai.

N: No need. You drink too much chai. Drink this *nariyal paani.*

Me: Arre, but I want chai.

N: Half a cup of *nariyal paani* won't kill you. Chalo.

Sigh. I drink the coconut water.

Me: There. Can I get chai now?

N: Loser. Okay.

Nazi now loves travel and food shows. She shakes her head at the soap dramas Aai watches. She has been to Kashmir, Shimla, Coonoor, Ahmedabad, Hyderabad, Goa, Kerala and Bhilai, and the recent owner of a brand new passport, has just returned from a trip to Thailand.

She knows that *dhaniya* is called 'coriander' and *paalak* is called 'spinach'. She travels only by flights, cabs and third AC. She started wearing bindis to ape my mom and then stopped wearing them because my toddler son kept eating them. She has graduated from only three-fourth sleeved salwar kameezes to half-sleeved ones with designed neckholes. She has started colouring her hair and investing her money. She even lent me money to buy my house and takes great pleasure in reminding me of the favour every time I act smart.

The house maids from all over the gully stash their savings in Nazi's drawer. They come to her to withdraw it regularly; she is meticulous in her accounts.

Sometime between me learning the meaning of *behooda* (shameless) and *oundhike* (blind) and her learning 'whatever' and 'so dumb', she has come to be part-owner of my mother's property and full-owner of all of us. And although she can't decide whether she is an aunt to my children or a grandmom, she has decided that she wants to be buried after she dies and that our children will inherit all her wealth. And even today, she threatens to quit.

# 8.

# Tring-Tring Comes the Telephone

The arrival of Nazia changed more than just our living habits. She changed a lot of our careless social habits too. In a house where curtains were just a formality, the intensely private Nazia actually started keeping doors and windows closed. She disliked us having to go to someone's house to answer the phone or to watch TV and somehow soon after her arrival, my parents started considering buying both, thereby changing our entire social dynamics. The first to arrive was the phone.

I must have been in third standard; Baba had come to pick me up from school. That in itself was a big thing. Because when Baba would come to school, I would take him straight to the canteen and point to popcorn or masala roll and cone ice cream. Which flavour? Why, chocolate of course. It cost Rs. 2.50 in those days. The orange/mango candy cost Rs. 1.50. Anyway, as we walked (me in my usual singsong style, hanging onto his hand, eating my ice cream), Baba dropped the bombshell.

Baba: There is a surprise for you at home.

Me: Really! What? New dress? High heels?

Baba: No. No. Even better.

Me (jumping up and down): What? What? What? Tell me na.

Baba managed to hold on till we reached our building. Then at the gate, as I rushed forward to check out for myself, he loudly announced, "It's a telephone."

I screeched, "Yahoo!" and hurried all the way home.

The telephone was a status-building acquisition.

It was a shiny green-grey machine with a round plastic dial. It was that rounded type of phone that came between the dull black clunky phones and the sleek rectangular ones. I touched the machine in excitement, reverence, wonder. I lifted the receiver; the phone was not yet connected. It would take seven days to connect the line and be able to make and receive calls. But that didn't matter. I dialled a number – 453053 – my grandmother's and then 396355 – my maushi's. Those were the only two numbers I knew by heart. Then I dialled 100. Aai immediately reprimanded, "Don't. You'll spoil the dial by turning it too fast. Stop fiddling with it."

What's the big deal about a phone? Really, if you were born with a telephone at your ear, there is really no big deal. But there I was. Everywhere I went, people had telephones; my kaki in Vasai (at that time Vasai was a trunk call) had a phone, my aunt in Grant Road had a phone and my grandparents in Shivaji Park had a phone. Villains or vamps talked to henchmen (for some reason, Hindi film heroes never did) all the time on these fancy looking red or yellow phones.

In those days, the big thing about phones was not the making of the call; it was the receiving. There was much authority in being summoned to the phone because someone was in need. There was that thrill in lifting the receiver and saying with authority, 'Hello.'

Phones were taken seriously. Nobody called to ask mundane insignificant things like, "Where have you reached?" or "What's up, man?". If people just wanted casual information about some person's well-being, they visited each other. They called only if it was a matter of great importance and urgency. Few of our society households did have a telephone but we didn't have symbiotic neighbourhood relationships with any of them. So we didn't receive many calls.

But then our phone arrived and soon our social worth rose. Immediately, the next-door Shirsats took our number; my mami

upstairs, whose calls came at the Prabhu household earlier, switched loyalties to us, even if it meant climbing down three storeys to answer one call.

For five days, my sister and I played with the dead phone. We pretended to be film heroines saying, "*Kyaaaa... nahi*" in that exaggerated tone and then collapsing on our knees while sobbing into the receiver. Sometimes we pretended that a killer was following us through the house and we were frantically trying to reach the phone to call the police. (As you can imagine, we devised many of these film scenario-inspired games: heroine-rushing-up-a-hill-to-commit-suicide or hero-mother-getting-shot type games). Or we just picked up the phone and sang songs into it. Every evening I came home from school, I asked chirpily, "Has it started yet? Can we make a call?"

Then finally in about a week, the phone started – just like that, on its own. Our parents were out and I guess it was the rainy season because we hadn't been allowed to play outside and so, my sister and I, Sai and Bali (the Nerurkar siblings from the fourth floor) were playing in our living room. Then during one of our phone games, we heard the dial tone. Boy, did we freak out! For some inexplicable reason, we immediately called 100.

The conversation went a bit like this:

Police control room: Namaskar, Mumbai Police room.

Four kids chortling: *Aye, tum police pandu hai.* (At that time, *pandu* was a big word; I think it meant buffoon.)

Police: Hello, who is speaking?

Again with more giggling: *Tum* stupid *hai*, idiot *hai*.

Police: Aye, who is speaking? Police will come and arrest you.

Sai (in a fit of bravado): *Tum padrya hai, tum hagrya hai.* (In plain speak, you are a farter, shitter.)

And then we quickly put the phone down and started laughing. The phone was working and we were the first to discover it. We told our parents as soon as they got home. And also about the phone call.

A more responsible parent would have been concerned about our delinquent behaviour or the deep-seated anti-establishment psyche we had displayed by calling the police *padrya*. But not our parents. They smiled widely and immediately dusted the phone. Mind you, they didn't make any calls.

That night, Sucheta maushi called, just on the off-chance that the phone line may have started working. My mum happily chatted with her. Our love affair with the phone had started.

For several months after that, the phone became an event in itself. My mum covered it with a pista green-and-white crochet lace and Baba bought a small lock for the dial (perhaps to avoid any more police calls, I suspect). In those days, the phone arrived with a local directory. And my mum and dad would sit with the directory, looking for phone numbers of family members and acquaintances to fill in a brand new, spiffy phone diary. Many arguments broke out over the system of entering the names alphabetically.

For instance:

Baba: Why have you written Dr. Deshmukh in D?

Aai: Then where should I write it? On your head?

Baba: Write it in L. We call him Lambya.

Aai: So what? You know that his name is Deshmukh.

Baba: Yes. If I need his phone number urgently, it is easier to look in L.

Aai (sarcastically): If you need his number urgently, ask me. I'll look it up in D for you.

Baba: Ch% ^ %ya.

Eventually Baba was proved right. Once Aai urgently needed Baabi maushi's number and called us from office to get it.

Aai (on the phone): Jaanu, look in the diary and tell me Baabi maushi's number.

Me: Wait. (Then after looking for it) It's not there.

Aai: How is that possible? Where are you looking?

Me: In B.

Aai: Why in B? *Adani* (illiterate). Look in P. Her surname is Pawar. I have written Baabi in brackets.

Me (as I sift through the pages): Not there.

Aai: Okay, then see in M. Her real name is Malti; I may have saved it there.

Me: Ummm no.

Aai: Look properly. Give it to Baba.

Baba (comes to the phone): *Bolo*. It is not there.

Aai: It's there. It's written with her US address.

Baba: It's not there. In M or P.

Aai: Leave it. I'll come home and find it.

She did eventually find it. But not where we were all looking. It was in B under the name of Bhaskar Power (which is the American version of their family name) with Baabi written in brackets.

The same confusion happened with people like Appaji (whose name was Madhukar Naik, but nobody in the family was aware of it) or even Baby maushi (Leena Verti, another family secret). Confusion reigned among Appe, Aake, Appa, Akka; there were two Vilas Samants, two Ratnakar Naiks, three Mohan kakas, two Mangals and hundreds of Samants. Oh well, after many such Baabi maushi situations, the tele-diary turned to forming its own system. So Appaji was in A, Baby maushi and Baabi maushi in B, Sushila and DG Nerurkar (my grandparents Aaji and Anna) in A, Suniti Samant in M for Mothi kaki and so on. It simplified life quite a lot.

The public directory was itself another avenue for new experiences for Baba. Sometimes he would pore over the pages looking for familiar names like Raj Kapoor or Dev Anand or Dharmendra; I don't know if he found them. He looked for old friends with whom he'd lost touch, then there'd be three options for a particular Khadilkar and he'd jot down the numbers, calling them one by one. None of the Khadilkars was the right one.

Then once detective Karamchand found one phone number as a clue on the television show. Baba immediately jotted down the number and called up as soon as the show was over, saying, "Let's find out who this number belongs to."

Baba: Hello is this 64-something-something?
(It was a Bandra number.)

Voice on the other side: Yes, who is speaking?

Baba (a little nervously): Hi, sorry to disturb but this number was telecast on *Karamchand* and we thought we would find out whom it belongs to.

The voice on the other side could well have told us to F-off or even just mind our own business. Instead:

Voice: Oh really, I must say you pay a lot of attention to *Karamchand*. I am Pankaj Parashar, director of the serial.

Baba: Oh really. This is your residence number? Glad to meet you. We love your serial (which was true). You are a brilliant director (which was an exaggeration, this was the first time Baba had ever heard of Pankaj Parashar.)

Voice: Oh yes. Thank you, thank you.

Baba: Oh yes, oh yes. Thank you sir.

Fade out. This conversation became a hot topic of social interactions. Then once, Baba even used that newfound friendship to call him and criticise some creative nuances of the thickening plot in *Karamchand* and how so-and-so shouldn't have been the culprit. I don't think that Mr. Parashar appreciated that much. Baba tried that with some other number on another show too but that didn't belong to anyone important.

Most of the ten years of her children's schooling, fourth floor's Mangal mami came after dropping her children at school to receive phone calls or make other correspondence or indulge in matchmaking on our phone. She'd bring with her other family gossip and news. When she had a squabble with the other next-door Patils or was long due to repay them some borrowed money, Seema *vahini* from right next door would come, smelling of dal and masalas, to make and receive calls at our place.

Baban kaka's wife would call to give her husband messages to bring some vegetables or coriander on the way back from work. Then, because staff from the Nishigandha garage just dropped in and called without offering to pay and we were too awkward to ask verbally but too *kadka* to let it go, within a year, we had a written notice asking people to pay Rs. 3 to make a call.

Slowly, people got their own telephones and social gossip became rare. But we had already become engrossed in our own lives and friends by then. As I grew into my teens, my fascination with the phone changed form. Homework and notes were exchanged on a call. Plans to meet friends were made on the phone. The telephone gave me a strange freedom. I could stay back longer at a friend's provided I called home and informed my parents. I made blank calls to secret crushes, mean teachers and so on. I received blank calls, sometimes a bold admirer or two, sometimes some dirty talk from a pervert.

For everyone, 449758 was our number, the identity of our mad family. It was the sole witness to all my private chats with my to-be, could-be, could-never-be and ex-boyfriends and a private observer of the break-up, patch-up dramas and crushes of my best friends as well. It was the number that conveyed my mother's first big Rajya Natya Parishad award for singing and my never-expected distinction in the SSC exams. Over the years, our number changed from 449758 to 4111858 to 24151858 to 24146777. Our family changed, as did all its members. Today we communicate in an entirely different way.

But the cellphone could never be what the landline was to our generation – an identity for the entire family, a single link to an entire ecosystem, all centred around one phone machine.

# 9.

# Samant Powder

Before the liberalisation of the '90s, kids of my generation were exposed to very few brands around us – Tata shampoo, Horlicks, Jai soap, Hamam, Rexona, Lux, Gold Spot and Thums Up. For the rest of our needs, we had to do with some really obscure products. Like Samant Powder.

A lot of my childhood evenings and holidays were spent at my grandmother's Shivaji Park house. These memories are bathed in the smell of Samant Powder. To give you an idea, my Aaji's house was huge and musty, like a museum. She had a big, heavy teak writing desk and a big three-way folding dressing table that had many, many small and big drawers and loads of old, fancy things inside it. My grandparents believed in conservation; they believed everything that had worn out or become useless could be reused for some entirely new purpose. So they 'saved' everything – heaps of visiting cards of all family members at various stages of their careers, coloured plastic visiting card boxes, printing colour samples, key rings with shade cards, paper cutters of different sizes, worn-out cricket gloves, staplers that didn't work, rusted staple pins, ball pens, used ball pen refills, notepads, leftover wedding invites of all their children, heaps of rubberbands, pencils, erasers, single bangles, earrings, chunky buttons, hippie finger rings, broken parts of leather belts, unused diaries from 1968, '72 or '82 and so on. They owned some really crazy stuff. They had two broken typewriters; we weren't allowed to touch either.

Anna, my grandfather, studied to be an advocate. He was quite a loser at it. Then he tried to be an entrepreneur, and he was a loser at that too. He started a polythene bag making unit in Panvel, which failed. Unfazed, he started an electrical fittings agency, which also failed. My grandparents' house was a sprawling 3BHK flat, with a separate dining room and huge balcony in Shivaji Park. But what made this place a true wonderland was one bedroom that was used exclusively to store Anna's failed business stock – namely raw balls or marbles of polythene which were used for making bags, heaps of small plastic bag samples (the kinds used for packaging say, masalas or earrings and so on), a mountain of tubelight fittings and what we call chokers (the object that jiggles the tubelight into behaving). These useless trinkets kept us children occupied for days on end.

It was like a fairyland of junk. And the fairy dust was Samant Powder. I am sure you have never heard of Samant Powder. Nobody has. But Anna-Aaji's store room had loads of Samant Powder boxes and dozens just lying around in drawers and cupboards.

It was a product manufactured, I suspect, by a crony of Anna's, one Mr. Bhende, clearly another loser at the business of talcum powder making. The man had made all this powder – I suspect he had packaged that powder in Anna's plastic polythene – and then when nobody bought it, he paid Anna for his plastic by giving him a decade's supply of his powder.

Samant Powder was a pale pink powder and smelled… oh, how do I describe its sharp, musty smell, its about-to-rot woody scent and its dull chemical overtones?

To give it its due, there must have been a time when it may have smelled fresh and flowery. That was the job of the talcum powder. But that era, and its fragrance, was long gone. Somewhere between lying in those lifeless plastic and big brown cardboard boxes, the two scents had mingled into one deadly smell.

In those days, talcum powder was the thing. I remember being constantly doused in it as a child.

In fact, we got dressed to go out in three easy steps:

**Step 1**. Wash hands, feet, face and neck.

**Step 2.** Change clothes.

**Step 3.** Pour talc liberally over one's arms, underarms, face, forehead and neck.

Unless my forehead, hair parting, ears, neck and the neckline of the dress had visible traces of talc, my mum would send me back again to get ready 'properly'. Everyone used to smell of Nycil in the summer and Ponds Dreamflower talc for the rest of the year.

Well, since there was all this powder lying around and my grandparents didn't believe in wastage, the whole extended family used this awful pink mixture. So intense was this pink that on most days Anna-Aaji looked like they had measles and when I used it on my own, Aai would always rub my face to check if it was a rash or just powder.

Probably because I must have been born to it, the musty odour of the Samant Powder has always been associated with Aaji-Anna in my mind. For some reason, they called it the 'khaki' powder.

Samant Powder was an incredible thing – this thing of great abundance, ubiquity and more importantly the only thing in that museum we could play with without being reprimanded or corrected. That's how, after lying inactive for years in those boxes, the Spowder started moving around the house, mutating. One would find it in strange places – in desk drawers with the pens, pencils and rulers, in the dressing table with the lipsticks and compact, even in cupboards among ironed clothes and in jewellery boxes.

As kids, we found many creative uses for it.

I must have been six and Swati tai (my partner in crime) was a couple of years older. Having discovered that talcum powder creates a slippery floor when sprinkled on tiles, Spowder was routinely used to secretly play skating-skating in Anna's store room. It made many a mighty take a great fall later and therefore, was the cause of many of the beatings we took.

Sometimes we would take a mug of water and pour quite a lot of pink powder and watch it float on the surface. Sometime we rubbed it all over the three-way folding mirror and wrote on it. Sometimes the Spowder acted as the gravy and atta in our kitchen while playing *ghar-ghar*. We could play Holi anytime with Spowder instead of *gulal*. It also helped as a prop in the witch game to de-witch the victim. Once we doused one full packet of the Spowder onto our hair and flung our hair this way and that to see how it formed a pink cloud around our heads. Of course, then Aaji noticed the mess on the bed and we got a sound beating!

At times we mixed this Spowder with water and applied the paste on our faces, then waited till it dried. I swear it made our faces softer, exactly like Afghan Snow Vanishing Cream.

Then once there was a rat menace in the house and for some inexplicable reason, they launched a vicious attack on the Spowder stock. It leaked out of the boxes in good measure; it spread in the gaps between the floor tiles, it stuck to the corners of the room, it sprinkled every time one shifted the boxes.

Slowly, even the elders were inspired by us. They started using the Spowder for non-conventional purposes – to sprinkle on the carrom board or inside the shoes to dry them out. I suspect Aaji even used it as an ant-repellant in later years.

In spite of this careless, wonderful wastage, Samant Powder lasted us for a fair amount of years, maybe five-six years. Even the younger sibling and cousins – Tanvi, Soorashree, Ameya, Vaidehi, Vallari and Alok – have a distinct memory of it. That is a long time to be using a talc. And this is a long time to remember its fragrance.

# 10.

# Idiots Around the Idiot Box

The arrival of the colour TV in the '80s was a redefining moment for our generation. Its entry in our house proved to be a redefining moment for our family.

The colour TV, our first and only, was our first big possession as a consumer. And it wouldn't be an exaggeration to say that it completely changed the ways of my family forever. For starters, it meant that we had become at the time fully self-sufficient socially.

Before the colour TV entered our lives, we used to go to the Shirsat's house in the evenings to catch some entertainment on their clunky black-and-white set. However, the Shirsats also had a foul-speaking irate grandfather who would shoo off children when it suited him.

A usual evening on Doordarshan in those days showed *Kamgar Vishwa* and *Kridangan* in Marathi, *Aao Maari Saathe* and *Santa Kukdi* in Gujarati and then Marathi News (which was mostly more exciting than the earlier entertainment programmes), followed by some prime-time entertainment and then English News. People switched on the TV exactly at 5.50 p.m. There would be a static colour bar and the melancholic Kaufmann-composed Doordarshan tune-in melody played on loop.

Is the picture tedha and wobbly?
Yes

A little later, Doordarshan started another channel, very innovatively called the Second Channel, which played *Giant Robot* on Mondays. This resulted in the very creative Giant Robot game too, where one person (the bad man) would follow the rest of the children and then we would talk into our imaginary watches to call Giant Robot to the rescue. General jumping and screaming would follow.

Television came to 1, Loukik when I was seven. It was a sturdy clunky grey ECTV. At the time, TV played a lot of foreign drama like *Old Fox* and the *DiDi's Comedy Show*. Doordarshan also started *Hum Log*, a drab soap opera about a large family struggling to make ends meet. The underlying message was about family planning, I think. Then there was *Buniyaad*, another educational saga about the Partition, which taught us that mums are called *Chaiji* in Punjabi. We never missed a single episode of *Nukkad, Subah, Idhar Udhar, Yeh Jo Hai Zindagi* or *Karamchand*. Characters like Ghanshu Bhikari, Khopdi and Tambi became an inspiration for our games. Karamchand's carrot-munching "Shut up, Kitty" was part of the school slang.

TV meant *Chitrahaar* and *Chhayageet* as well. Our home always had a Ram Bharose Hindu Hotel kind of ambience. My mum woke up with *Akaashwani* and *Vividh Bharati* and fell asleep with *Bela Ke Phool* or *Bhule Bisre Geet* in the background. And so these film song programmes were right up her alley. And I loved the whole song-and-dance routine. During these programmes, I'd dance and swing to the songs like the heroine did, with a dupatta on my head. If my dad was home, I'd ask him to be the hero and dance around him.

Of course, my heartless parents had no appreciation for my interest in the arts. They'd just ask me to dance out of the way of the television.

It is understandable I suppose. This is what happens when two generations discover something momentous like television together. My parents were as thrilled about the idiot box as we kids were. They wanted to open the TV set, touch the screen, trace their hand on the scary hump behind, try the plugs, the knobs.

The TV totally changed our family life.

After the arrival of television, we ate all our dinners in front of the set. My parents covered it with a lacy table cloth, put the user booklet in a safe place; they worshipped it on Dussehra by putting a tika and flower on it. They even stored the box and thermocol in the loft! And then because they were so in awe of it, they forbade us from touching it or watching it without them.

"Oh did you see how that five-year-old was touching the knobs on the television set? No manners," my parents would say when they returned from a household where kids were allowed to touch the television.

In the beginning, my sister and I could only switch on the TV under parental guidance. Then they made up some myths around the idiot box to keep us further away. Like these:

**Myth 1.** TV will spoil your eyes if you watch it from too close.

**Myth 2.** TV doesn't have real stories. But those characters can come out of the set and do something bad to you. So do not start the TV when nobody is at home.

**Myth 3.** Watching TV makes you go cross-eyed. (My mother said that about the Sadhna fringe cut too.)

**Myth 4.** If you watch it for too long at one go, the TV will heat up and explode!

**Myth 5.** If you turn the knob too hard, it'll come off in your hand.

**Myth 6.** There is a certain age when you become eligible to touch a TV, you know, like driving. It is okay for adults to do anything with a TV.

You'd be forgiven for thinking that my parents were manipulative. But I think that they believed most of these myths themselves. My mother fanatically covered our TV screen for many long years. She still warns us to not stand too close to it and will not watch it for more than a couple of hours at a go. She'll say, "*TV la thanda hou de.*" (Let the TV cool down a bit.)

At times it was rather silly really. My dad would unplug the TV before he left for his dispensary in the evening so we wouldn't watch it and do our homework instead. My ma would return from work and want to switch it on (to watch Marathi news!) and wouldn't know how to. I'd help her out by plugging it in. And Baba would not know any better.

Television brought entertainment to our crazy household in more ways than one. Mainly it become a source of occupation for my frisky father. Baba had a rare TV-related obsessive compulsive *keeda* to tinker with things. Now, TV sets in those days didn't have a remote control but a manual tuning system. This required a person to sit right in front of the set and turn that small orange stick (it was THE most carefully kept item in our house) in the channel knob to correct or finetune the picture quality.

Now just when a programme started to get interesting, Baba would decide that the picture quality wasn't too good and stand right in front of the TV set and start fiddling around with the picture.

Many of my visual memories of TV programmes consist of a human's back in the foreground and incessant arguments which went a little like this:

Me/Tanu (in outrage): Baba, move out of the way. There is nothing wrong with the picture.

Baba: What nonsense. See these lines in the picture.

Me/Tanu (in frustration): Baba yaar pleeeese, the picture is fine.

Baba: Arre you just see what a difference this will make.

(More fiddling that actually worsens the picture)

Me/Tanu (screaming): Baba, you have spoiled it now. We can't see anything.

Baba (sheepishly, moving out of the way): There is some problem with the antenna upstairs. Will repair it this Sunday.

Tuning seemed to give my father a sense of control and achievement. As if he was preparing that picture for us, you know, like telling a story or singing a song. Like many fathers who change bulbs at home or clean or fix the car or do some such useless activities on lazy Sunday mornings, my Baba would make a big production of adjusting the TV antenna (after he was back from buying the chicken for Sunday lunch, that is). He would bring home the chicken, have a long bath, stride out smartly smelling of eau de cologne, climb four storeys to the terrace, clean the antenna with a dry cloth, then fiddle with it, shift it this way and that. I would be stationed in front of our main door on the ground floor, looking at the picture on the TV. I had to shout out to him when the picture started improving or worsening. Then he'd fiddle some more and shout back. The conversation went something like this:

Me: No, no, no. Baba, shift the antenna. The picture is not clear.

Baba: Okay, check now.

Me: It's still not clear.

Baba: What nonsense, see again. It must be clear.

Me: It is still not clear, Baba.

Baba: Are there lines on the screen? Or is the picture *tedha*

and wobbly?

Me: *Tedha* and wobbly.

Baba jiggles the antenna some more.

Baba: Okay, now check.

Me: Uh huh. Not good. It is worse than earlier now.

Baba: You're a ch$%**ya *saala*. See properly.

Me: Fine then. You see for yourself.

I go back home in a huff. Baba climbs down in a huff and checks the picture himself.

Baba: This is not a wobbly picture. It is *tedha*. You are giving me wrong information.

Me: I am not. This picture is wobbly. See, it is wobbling.

Baba: You don't know anything.

He goes right back up and repeats the same process till the picture is brought back to the original quality. This nicely takes up a couple of hours and gets Baba out of Aai's hair.

This often resulted in peaceful Sunday mornings for us. After the advent of *Ramayan* and *Mahabharat* on Sunday mornings, this practice had to be postponed to after the telecast of the mythological serials.

TV also wrought a change in our social habits. From a family that went to the neighbour's home to watch TV, we became one with a TV. That considerably changed our social dynamics.

In those days, TV was a collective experience. It brought people together and it kept them arguing together. Our society was divided by the haves and have-nots. Elders watched *Phool Khile Hai Gulshan Gulshan* together or children watched *Giant Robot* at somebody's house. Owning a TV gave people a sense of power. When neighbours fought, with frantic hand-wringing and finger pointing, TV-owners said, "Three years I have shown her TV at my house and see how she is talking now." And they were told in return, "Arre, I can afford 56 TVs like yours. Just you see, if I don't get a bigger and better TV in six months, I'll change my name."

Television was also a medium with the power to heal. Some months later, the same TV owner would go to invite the said neighbour and TV guest for his daughter's wedding, then slip in an apologetic invite for TV viewing too. And the person would be back watching TV in the same household as if nothing happened, both imagining that they were doing the other a big favour.

In our home, TV fulfilled a larger social service purpose too. Let me explain how.

Everybody knows what big weekly events *Ramayan* and *Mahabaharat* were. In our household, their weekly telecasts were social events like a weekly Mahapuja or Mahayagna. At the time, the whole entertainment-starved city came to a nail-biting stop as Rama fought his enemies slowly – arrow by arrow, spark by spark – and Ravindra Jain howled in the background with ecstatic devotion. I think, three episodes went as a prelude to Draupadi's *vastraharan* and the actual act went on in six-yard detail for a full episode.

Our living room window faced the road and on occasion of all cricket matches, many roadside loafers often sat on the mandir compound wall, looking into our TV set through our window.

During *Ramayan* and *Mahabharat*, the whole of the patient-population – cancer patients and families who had come from villages all over the country to convalesce at the Shree Gadge Maharaj Dharamshala for the sick and terminally ill in front of our building – would congregate in our house to watch TV. The women sat in our living room, with their strong and sweet chameli hair oil and musty cotton saree smells, while the men stood outside in our building compound and in the Ganpati temple to catch the action through the window.

It was quite a bother. For one, we had to wake up, eat and have our baths by 9.30 a.m. on a Sunday because that's when the hordes would arrive. Then, we had to be all decent and sit demurely (you know with our legs together tucked under us). And we couldn't make our standard loud Samant comments during the serial!

But it was nice in other ways. Every week, patients would come and go, sometimes back to their villages and lives, sometimes to the crematorium. And with the regulars, we formed a friendship, awkward but warm. They'd give us a weekly update on their patient's health (although Baba was a dentist, many people from the dharamshala brought their reports to him for an opinion) or smile and tell us that the *kathore ilaaj* (chemo) is finally over.

Eight-year-old leaukemic Kamlesh's mother came complaining about the Marwadi dharamshala's vegetarian policy and the doctor's prescription to eat eggs. My mum promptly offered to boil eggs or cook omelettes for him everyday.

The old *dehati* woman with the curly white post-chemo mop of hair and the single breast would talk of her hopes of finishing her therapy and rushing to her village for her third daughter's marriage. And then coming back with an album to show us the pictures.

The young woman with the big eyes, bright red *sindoor* and inch-thick kajal would talk about her husband's grumpiness and mistreatment after his leg amputation and then about her impatience with his clumsiness with his new artificial limb.

It was just casual chit-chat for them but it often filled me with questions. And my parents with worry.

"Baba, what is chemotherapy?"

"Will she feel better?"

"Why is she looking worse even with treatment?"

"Is he going to die?"

Aai would ask Baba the details of a report after someone came for an informal consultation post dinner someday. And Baba, a normally forthcoming and blunt person, would shake his head or shrug.

It became difficult to tell if someone not returning from their hometown after a gap was good news or bad news. If they returned, they would return the favour of watching TV in our house by bringing *gajak* or *petha* or some equally awful mithai. A *tabela* owner would bring a small dabba of ghee; Kamlesh's father, who was a cobbler, once brought us pretty *mojris* (he eventually absconded with his son's treatment money during his son's third chemo cycle!); an old woman would bring red glass bangles or a cotton saree for Aai.

We had always been taught to look at the thought behind the gift. But never before had I imagined that people could be so thoughtful even in their abject misery, poverty and grief. The dynamics of giving and taking became so much clearer to us. They sought reassurance in us. And when they returned, even if for a repeat chemo, along with their sweets, they also brought hope to us that they were alive and willing to fight.

The dharamshala now has its own TV and my dad is no longer alive to dispense free medical advice but patients still come to us for used pillows, bedsheets, milk, sugar to make tea, sometimes to get some spices ground in our mixer and sometimes to share the good news of their relative's complete recovery. In that sense, the TV has been truly a window to reality. For a brief, short-lived phase, the television also made us a normal family, who sat in a room watching TV without arguing. But only till the emancipating video came along. Now that was one thing that gave me unprecedented powers in my own household and went on to mould my adolescent personality.

# 11.

# How the VCR Changed My Life

*Betaab* was the first film I saw on video. I was six. It was on my cousin Beena tai's building terrace in Parel; all the youngsters in the building had contributed to collectively rent the video on the day the film released. I slept off during the first half of the film, but the other young adults went on to watch three-four films back to back.

Over the next couple of years, the VCR became a highly empowering gadget for my generation. For the generation before mine, film viewing was not something families did together. Theatres were places you went to with your friends, never your parents. Films were considered either corruptive or frivolous. School dropouts and jobless people went to the cinemas, my grandmother would say. My grandfather, Nana ajoba, had never seen a film till his late sixties. Although my parents saw their own share of matinees, it was always without the knowledge of their parents. It was strictly forbidden in their day and my parents generally were of the opinion that we could very well do without all the things that they did without. I must have seen about 11 films in a theatre from my birth till the time I entered college: four of them with my parents, two with our kiddie group from the building and the rest with Nazi. *Aazadi Ki Ore*, *Naache*

VCR

*Mayuri, Chhota Chetan 3D, Tarzan* and *Qayamat Se Qayamat Tak* are some of them. We watched these films in a theatre within a one-kilometre radius from home. And we went to watch the film only after the rest of the world had seen it and suggested we go for it.

The point of all of this is to establish that I come from a film-starved generation. What happens when you give a film-starved generation – whose only regular fix of films is restricted to the annual Ganesh festival street-side screenings and the Saturday/Sunday evening telecast on Doordarshan – a gadget that can not only screen films in their own homes or localities but watch them as many times as they want? They go complete bonkers, that's what.

My generation appropriated the video from the very beginning; even when we were renting it, we claimed it as our own, and soon built it up into a must-have commodity for fun gatherings. By the time I was eight, we had convinced our parents that if they wanted us noisy kids out of the way at any social gathering, all they had to do was just rent a video cassette player for a night.

We were allowed this on the condition that we could watch only children's films on it. Yes, the children's films condition was a bit much. But in the '80s, the concept of a children's film was quite flexible.

a. A children's film means one that should have children in it. So it could be a *Mr. India*, which was genuinely a kiddie flick. But it could also be a *Masterji*, where Sridevi pranced around with a couple of kids to *patao* the widowed teacher Rajesh Khanna. It could also be a *Rakhwala*, a solid Anil Kapoor *tapori* action film, but with a bunch of orphaned roadside children. Or an *Aaj Ke Angaarey*, where Archana Puran Singh is a school teacher in a hot pink mini skirt and short midriff and cleavage showing jacket. The outfit was otherwise unremarkable, except that the girl crouched sexily behind a bus with a dozen or so school kids or crawled through an underground cave running away from masked men for around 80 per cent of the film. This film intrigued us – that school teachers could be this hot and wear unmentionable things and still retain their jobs and children's respect, that school children could be kidnapped when they went on a trip and that they could fight powerful looking men all by themselves. We saw the film on video on the first weekend of its release and by the second week, knew its songs by heart.

b. If there are no children, it should have animals in it. There was a general opinion that films that starred animals were actually children's films. Talking monkeys, nodding and jumping elephants, fiercely communicative dogs, vengeful snakes or supernatural things were big with us. Such films won instant approval from parents. That's how we ended up getting permission to watch *Tarzan* in the theatre and also a lot of the *Haathi Mere Saathi* type of fare. There was a Mithun film, *Shikari The Hunter*, which starred a Russian beauty queen of the time, with lots of animals from a circus, which we hugely enjoyed. We must have watched Wonder Dog Brownie Moti's fight scenes in *Teri Meherbaniyan* some five times; Brownie Moti avenges his master's girlfriend's rape and death and master's murder all by himself. We would rewind and watch Sridevi's eyes changing colours in *Nagina* over and over again and we saw its sequel *Nigahen* on the Friday it released. Not to mention that we played the Naagin version of Catch-the-Cook, a game where one had to be a Naagin and slither on the floor to catch others running in the room.

As you can see, we saw a lot of the '80s trash. At the beginning, a video player rental cost Rs. 250 for a night. And people made the most of it by watching three-four films back to back (the last film was usually forwarded in huge chunks because the videowala would be cooling his heels outside, waiting to take the video player back.) The video cassette rental would be Rs. 12 for a film in the first week of its release, Rs. 10 for a new film and Rs. 8 for an old film.

In those days, it didn't matter which film you saw, as long as you saw one. The ambition was in the numbers, not in the quality. We'd go to school after a social outing and boast about the number of films we saw there all night. We'd watch an old happy family film, say *Junglee*, or *Kashmir Ki Kali* or *Half Ticket*, to appease the elders. Then once they finished their film and became sleepy, we'd put on the most exciting film of the night, say a *Saagar* or *Teri Meherbaniyan* or *Arjun* or *Hero* or *Hatya* and then end with a film like *Amar Akbar Anthony* or *Namak Halal* or *Geraftaar* and so on, which were okay enough to sleep through. If it was a holiday and the videowala didn't return to claim his equipment, we'd watch some parts of the films again. Sometimes the older cousins would secretly show us some version or the other of *Evil Dead*, *Nightmare on Elm Street*, *Omen* or some Ramsay saga like *Bandh Darwaza* or something and then our parents would wonder why we would not go to the bathroom without their supervision.

The video proved to be an instrument of character formation for me. For starters, it opened up my social life considerably. There were weekly invitations which were only meant for children: "Megha's renting a video this weekend. They are trying to get *Mohabbat*. Can I go?" "Manu kaka's girls are renting a video this Friday. I'm going." If there were no exams or school the next day, my parents generally had no hang-ups.

Soon I began to have contacts in the local cassette libraries. From Naigaum Dadar to King's Circle, I started sourcing titles, negotiating rates or rental times for the local gang of kids. I was the friend of *kaaniya* (the cross-eyed fellow) in Latest Circulating Library and he would allow me to keep an old cassette for over a week. I knew the pockmarked Irani of City Video Library and he'd keep special unopened, new titles reserved for me. And I made a friend whose father had a stake in Abbas Library at King's Circle where I could pay after watching the film and returning the tape.

I also realised I possessed a rare gift. Not only did I have the appetite to watch any trash dished out to me, but also the ability to guess – by just looking at the video cassette cover – whether a certain film would be entertaining or not. For instance, I had warned everyone that *Loha* would be an awful film, even with all that heavyweight star cast. But they wanted to see the Bombay Dyeing model act; it turned out to be a super-bore where Karan Kapoor trotted like a horse in songs and Dharmendra caught flying bullets in his hand.

Even *Pighalta Aasman*. Whatever does the title mean? It had an ageing Shashi Kapoor and Rakhee romancing and it really turned out to be a loser. I'd warned everyone to not let the music of *Dance Dance* fool them; the film had an actress crooning '*Zoobi Zoobi*' while she's being molested by Amrish Puri and Smita Patil in disco finery and frilly red skirts singing, '*Aa gaya aa gaya halwa wala aa gaya*'.

Govinda and Mandakini's *Pyar Mohabbat* was not the film it was meant to be. It has a *suhaag raat* song with Mandy in a transparent nightie and Nirodh condoms floating in the air. Really! I requested people to trust my instinct on Govinda's *Hatya* and it turned out to be a really good thriller. Gradually, my friends started trusting my superior judgement.

Because of this newfound ability and confidence, I started being respected. Friends in the gully called me to make important decisions like which dress to wear at a birthday party or what song to dance to at the gully's record dance competition and I became an important member of the panel which chose films, even if the video was not rented for my own house.

But more importantly, the video player also deepened the generation gap between me and my parents wonderfully. As pre-teens, we soon mastered the video; we learnt how to make it work for us and then we hypnotised our parents into believing that we would behave forever, we would study diligently, we would clean our drawers every week, if we only had a video recorder at home. We convinced them that we needed this special gadget to keep our family together and happy.

The arrival of the video player changed the power dynamics at home too.

The antenna adjustment ritual on Sundays was supplemented by the weekly video head-cleaning ritual. Of course, my Baba didn't do the tame, human thing by inserting a head-cleaning cassette. He would unscrew the video open and blow into it, then open the petrol tank of our scooter parked in our building garage, hand me a soft cloth and ask me to run to the scooter, dip the cloth into the petrol and run back and hand it to him. He'd clean the head and tell me to repeat the process. I don't know how that worked but that was how we did it. We used acetone or Old Spice even on our audio systems.

Suddenly, there were a host of things my sister and I could discuss without our parents having a clue. It gave us space and a standing in our family. My mother would hum some song and ask me which film it was from. I'd answer correctly and she'd wryly comment, "If you paid that much attention to your studies, you'd be a topper." I didn't take her comments to heart. She needed me to switch on the video after all.

Simply speaking, the video helped us take over the reins of entertainment in the family. If we thought a certain film was boring, we'd simply say it was unavailable at the cassette library or that the tape was faulty. My parents waited for me to get home to play the film they wanted. I got to play snobbish, dilly-dally a bit and then play the video for them.

On a quiet weeknight, Baba would ask, "Jaanu, so how was *Mohabbat*? Did you like it?" And I would say, "What a solid film it was!" and go on to narrate the full story, with all its songs and background music, till he nodded off to sleep.

Sunny Deol, Jackie Shroff, Sanjay Dutt, Kumar Gaurav were big but our parents were more peaceful with say Shammi Kapoor or Kishore Kumar or Rishi Kapoor or Jeetendra. We liked all of the *dhishoom-dhishoom* but they liked family dramas, so most household film rental choices were based on who the hero was and whether there was too much violence in it. So we settled for films like *Pyar Ka Mandir, Gharana, Ghar Ek Mandir, Sunny, Disco Dancer*, or *Kaash* that would work for both parents and kids. Not only did we see this trash, we saw it several times over.

To their credit, when the parents entered the fray, our film viewing became a little discerning. Baba introduced me to Walt Disney, Danny Kaye, Alfred Hitchcock and the Marx Brothers, Steven Spielberg, Clint Eastwood, Gregory Peck, Vijay Anand, even Bimal Roy. When we first scoffed at Dev Anand, calling him an oldie, Baba brought home *Johny Mera Naam* and *Jewel Thief* and changed our minds about him forever.

I don't think Baba paid a lot of attention to parental guidance instructions though. Watching *Psycho* and *Jaws* forever biased my mind against showers and the sea. I watched films like *Poltergeist, Platoon, The Birds, MacKenna's Gold* at a really tender age. That's what gave me the courage to see Manoj Kumar's *Clerk* or Kishen Kumar's *Aaja Meri Jaan* much later.

Video also brought our family closer. Many of these home screenings would be interspersed with Baba's or Aai's anecdotes on when they first saw the film in the theatre. How Sucheta maushi's friend came out of a *Teesri Manzil* screening and bumped into Aai and maushi as they entered Minerva theatre and exclaimed, "Arre what a *mast* film. Till the end, no one realises that Prem Nath is the killer!" Or how Baba and his dental college friends screamed out aloud, "PISSCO" when the title of *Psycho* played at Regal. Or how Baba wore his elder brother Tatya kaka's brand new grey woollen trouser when he went to watch *Guide*. On the way back, Tatya kaka spotted him from the other side of the busy road on Tilak Bridge and shrieked in anger.

Baba of course fled even as Tatya kaka shouted some obscenities at him. Or how an admirer asked my mum out for a film, *Paraya Dhan*, and she took along her younger sister and forced her to sit between the two of them throughout the film.

Sometimes the parents pulled the seniority card and asked for films like *Dr. Kotnis ki Amar Kahani* or *Sangam* or *Arth* or *Dil Ek Mandir* (they even said Arth was an adults only movie!).

The list goes on and on. As was to be expected, watching this much meaningless cinema completely corrupted my mind. I became one of those film buffs who wanted to become an actress. If I lived out of Bombay, I would have run away from home to come here and become an actress. Thankfully, destiny and my parents intervened.

# 12.

# The Frustrated Child Artist

By the time I was nine, I was sure that I wanted to get into show business. I dreamed of becoming a Hindi film heroine, getting dressed in baggy tops and tight jeans, wearing big round earrings and bright red lipstick. And I wanted frizzy permed hair. Frequent discussions with Baban kaka and Damu kaka and watching that much video had short-circuited my brain.

My few early attempts at getting onstage or on-screen were quite ill-fated. When I was around five, my slightly amused parents decided to do something about my constant preening in front of the mirror. In those days, when Maharashtrian parents wanted their daughter to learn some dance or song skill, they enrolled her in Sulabha and Arvind Deshpande's Avishkar workshops.

The Avishkar theatre group, which produced the musical *Durga Zhali Gauri*, trained young girls and boys in song and dance at a workshop in Chhabildas High School and then selected many of these participants for their production every year. I was rejected at this audition at the first go.

I came back crying because the workshop had ended and I was told to not come from the next day. I should have seen the writing on the wall.

Instead, I foolishly persisted with my acting aspirations. When I was in the sixth standard, I went on to participate in the auditions for the annual school play. That also turned out to be a tragedy. I got selected for a supporting role and rehearsals started. But two days later, the teacher arbitrarily told me to not come for rehearsals anymore because my voice wasn't 'proper'. She had found another student to replace me. I remember feeling devastated and crying my eyes out on the way home.

Baba (taking one look at my distraught face and tears at the door): What happened Jaanu?

Me: Sniff, sniff

Baba: Arre what happened?

More sniffing.

Baba: Why don't you say? Are you hurt?

Me: I... I... the teacher... I...

Baba (angrily): Calm down first. Did the teacher hit you? Did she threaten you? Were you caught copying? (That was the ultimate sin for my parents.)

Me (sniveling even more): No. Minal teacher replaced me in the play.

Baba: Oh, so why are you crying like someone has died?

Me: I want to act. But they won't take me.

Baba (getting angry at my disappointment): So that was not the only play in the world. Stop crying. If you want to act, you will. Let's figure out how to do this.

True enough, within a week Baba had cut out an ad for a Ramnath Tharval acting workshop and I was sitting in a circle learning to wiggle my eyebrows to express anger and shock. Although I was too young for the cut-off age for the workshop, Baba had pleaded with the teacher to give me a chance and take me on.

After the second class, when Baba was walking me back home, he asked me how it was.

Baba: So Jaanu, how was your acting class?

Me: Hmmm, okay.

Baba: Okay means? What did you do? Was it exciting?

Me: Hmm, not exciting or anything. So far, we have only learnt some exercises and how to move eyebrows and ears and stretch our face muscles. Nothing related to acting.

Baba: Arre, moving eyebrows is related to acting only. Haven't you seen K N Singh? You'll be a great actor if you know how to move your eyebrows menacingly like him. He was so talented. You know who K N Singh was?

Ahem. I didn't know who K N Singh was but I knew that I did not want to act like him. After I knew, I was sure. Truly speaking, that kind of acting wasn't what I had in mind. This workshop was like asking to read a poem and being handed the Bhagwad Gita.

I was thinking Parveen Babi and Tina Munim while my parents were thinking Shabana Azmi and Deepti Naval. All I wanted was a chance to dress up in lacy, frothy things, lots of goop and lipstick; they were thinking National School of Drama kind of acting – the internalising, the *navarasas*, the body language and all that. And the first play the workshop concluded with was a street play about protecting the environment and we all had to wear khadi kurtas and jeans with a dupatta tied to our waists! That was definitely not what I had in mind.

Some tiny roles happened after that workshop but unfortunately none of them were glamorous. Aai acted in some productions for her company BES&T (the Brihanmumbai Electricity Supply and Transport Company) and I was always the bit-role child artist. Once Aai took me for a rehearsal of her play at Rang Bhavan.

Me: Where are we going?

Aai: You wanted to act na? There's a small role for you.

Me: How small? Do I have dialogues? Will I play a princess?

Aai: No. It is of a small girl. But you'll have to learn to say your lines well. You won't be scared na?

Me: No. But is there make-up?

Aai: No.

Me: Shee, then I don't want to do it.

Aai: Keep quiet. Just do as I say.

It was the role of a street urchin asking for the price of a doll in a shop and being driven away by the shopkeeper! But there was make-up and I was quite excited by it.

Me (addressing the make-up artist): What will you put on my face?

Artist: This pancake to smoothen your face.

Me: Then you'll put lipstick?

Artist (laughing): No, no, no. You are a poor girl in the play. You can't wear lipstick.

Me: Rouge on my cheeks?

Artist: Uh huh (while doing up my face).

Me (shrieking as he applied a black line on my face): What is that?

Artist: This way you'll look poor.

Me (wail): I don't want to look poor.

Artist: Laugh, laugh, laugh

Determined not to give in, I appealed (with that one tear in my eye and a lip wobble): At least put a little lipstick.

Artist: Okay, here is a little colour for your lips. And here is a chocolate. Now run.

They let me keep the doll from the play and I suppose it was worth it.

Then my mother acted in a *sangeet natak* (musical drama), *Sangeet Kanhopatra*, in which they needed some kids to create a crowd for the *warkari yatra*. So there I was again, dressed in a ragged *parkar-polka*, holding a flag and shouting, "Vitthal, Vitthal, Vitthal".

Well, I went along with it. I still believed that I could become a glamorous actress at some point. I indeed got a break soon enough. My cousin had suggested my name to a director, who wanted to cast a young girl in a period drama about the first educated woman in India, *Pandita Ramabai*, and I was called to audition for the role of the young Pandita. I was very excited; I started visualising rich, shiny *parkar-polkas* and lots of jewellery and long hair (which meant a wig because my mum always kept my hair short).

Aai took me to meet Vaidya Sir, who was the principal of a prominent school in Goregaon. He practised some lines with me and I was selected. I was very excited; in the audition there was a dialogue where my brother asked me why I was so dressed up. It was a periodical and Vaidya Sir asked my mother to figure out a *parkar-polka* and some jewellery. This was my chance, I figured.

But this role was also not what it was touted to be. When full-fledged rehearsals started, I realised that just after the five minute well-dressed part, Pandita Ramabai's family goes through many hardships, poverty and a famine. So it was back to the rags and begging!

But the play proved to be the most enlightening experience of my nine-year-old life.

*Pandita Ramabai* turned out to be a play presented by the famous Stree Mukti Sanghatana. This women's organisation performed this play alongside well-known, famous musicals such as *Hunda Nako Ga Bai* (I Don't Want Dowry; a play about the evils of dowry) or *Mulgi Jhali Ho* (It's a Girl-Child; a play to support the cause of the girl-child) on women's issues. And after my performance in the play, they also made me wear the kurta and jeans with a dupatta tied at the waist and talk about gender equality across small towns in Maharashtra.

I think audiences in the interiors of Maharashtra found it terribly exciting that a nine-year old talked about feminism and all that.

I remember being quizzed and encouraged to speak at *mahila mandal* gatherings in Sangli, Latur, Beed and Parbhani to support the cause. *Pandita Ramabai* took me to shows all over Pune, Nasik, Palghar, Marathwada and Vidarbha in an ST bus, stopping at dormitories or government or college rest houses and performing, doing morchas and street plays in different areas.

It was my first time away from home without my parents and I must say I had quite a good time. Sharda (Sathe) maushi, Jyoti (Mhapsekar) maushi and Usha (Vaidya) maushi were my guardians and the whole group of youngsters was quite fond of me. I would earn a chocolate or an ice-lolly whenever anyone went for a cigarette and even if it were the rural hotspots of Maharashtra, I did get to travel quite a bit.

But to come back to my point, my fledgling career in showbiz was still going nowhere. And the time I got a role in *Kamgar Vishwa*, a Doordarshan series about labour class issues and rights, is when I finally accepted that there was a serious disconnect between my glamorous aspirations and my parents' understanding of what I wanted.

Aai: One of my theatre colleagues is doing a television series.

After the *Ramabai* episode, I knew better.

Me: What is the role?

Aai: It is about a poor girl studying to be a nurse.

Me: I don't want to be poor. Why do you always find such roles for me?

Aai: Arre, what can I do? People will give you roles only according to how you look.

Me: You mean I look poor?

Aai: No, but you are so scrawny. You look like you have not eaten a decent meal in ages. What can we do?

That was true. It was the age of the chubby child artist like Baby Guddi. All the roles went to girls with chubby cheeks. I was way too scrawny. Also, I think, although my parents wanted me to prove something to myself with this stint, they were very wary of upsetting my studies or seem as if they were actively seeking roles for me. In fact they were careful to ensure that none of my work was paid work. Film and television audition requests that came after Tharval's workshops were politely refused and I suspect I was allowed to work only with people and crews they were familiar with. Even so.

Me: But I don't want to do such roles. Why can't you find better roles? I want to become like Hema Malini.

Aai (with consternation): Whaaaat? Hema Malini hasn't studied anything.

Me: Fine then. Reena Roy (yeah, I know… but her side-ponytail and pedal-pushers were quite cool, I thought.)

Aai: She is not well-educated either.

Me: Padmini Kolhapure.

Aai: Not educated.

Me: What does that have to do with acting?

Aai: Everything. Do you want to do these couple of TV episodes or no? Anyway, in three-four years, you'll have to start concentrating on your studies. Your scores aren't looking too great. If you want to get into a good college, we are going to have to start pretty early.

Oh, well. There I was on the Doordarshan set.

TV sets smell peculiar; you remember the smell of Joker gum or Fevicol? Well, mix that with fresh paint and pancake and you'd arrive at the smell of a set. I don't know if lighting technology has changed much in the last two decades but TV sets are also very hot, uncomfortable places.

The Doordarshan building is very impressive from the outside. Baba would often show me the TV tower in Worli; in those days it was very much visible from our Loukik building terrace. In the Doordarshan premises, one could see the tower right up there in its full glory. At the time, the office had that big spiral logo right in the front, making it a familiar place. However, the insides of the studio were dinghy, bright and dark, noisy and silent, all at the same time. And the make-up smelt

strange too; it was cakey and sticky. For some reason, they called it pancake, although it didn't smell like any bakery item. It smelt like oil colours.

My mother took me to meet the director, an employee of the BES&T, who was doing this show part-time. However, he took one look at me and shook his head. He touched my short hair and said, "She needs a wig."

I was supposed to play a village girl and the plot was all about this poor girl wanting to study further and become a nurse. But in the show, her poor and illiterate parents keep forcing her to bunk classes and go do domestic work. Now, village girls have long hair and I didn't. So the make-up artist got busy. Some hundred pins were pierced into my scalp and a ghastly wig with two pigtails was fixed to my head in such a manner that I couldn't move or shake my head without experiencing extreme agony. (It made me understand why Sharmila Tagore was so slow and coy; she must not have been able to turn her huge wig-bearing head without turning her whole body.)

Make-up artist (surveying the wig on me from a distance) telling an assistant director and my mum, who were rehearsing my lines with me: It's too big for her head no?

I tried turning my head to see in the mirror. But I think some pins were fixed into my neck too. And the wig was too heavy.

Make-up artist: She can't move her head.

Assistant director: That's okay, she doesn't have to move it. She just has to look sad. And ha, she has to look up once.

Make-up artist: But she's looking pained.

Assistant director: That's even better. She's poor and has to do hard, physical labour. She needs to look like that.

Make-up artist: Hmm. (Adding some finishing touches) Then she's ready.

In a shooting though, getting an actor ready is neither here nor there. They first need everything else ready: the lights, the sound, the set, the camera, so on and so forth. So I sat there, resting my heavy head against a tall armchair, dangling my feet, watching them get things in order. It was uncomfortable, but I didn't mind it.

Then it was time to face the camera and that's when things started getting tricky.

Director: Lights. Camera. Action.

Now in the scene I was supposed to be cleaning utensils and cast a long, wishful dreamy look at my master's son studying. Then I was to look away and start saying my dialogues. But before I began…

Director: Cut.

A questioning look – from me and his assistant.

D (telling the assistant): She's too fair. She's too fair.

Assistant: But you have seen her before.

D: Yes, but she's looking too fair with the lights. She's supposed to come from a poverty-stricken family. She looks like she's come from an educated household.

Personally, I thought that wasn't such a bad thing to look like, especially if one was indeed from an educated family. But there was nothing I could do about this particular problem, especially since I had been selected in an audition and they should have thought of this earlier.

Assistant: Okay. So now what do we do?

They murmured solutions and tried to adjust the lighting. But the parents and the child, who were supposed to be my masters, were far darker than I was.

Take again.

Director: Lights, camera, action.

Again, the long wishful dreamy look. Then just as I looked away and start saying my dialogues:

Director: Cut.

Assistant: What happened?

Director: Too fair.

They suggested exchanging my role with another small, more impoverished looking girl in the serial, but she was to play a much longer role in the series and I couldn't play that role because that would have required more time for the shooting.

Given that the director was no Spielberg, they decided they would colour my face darker and get on with it. My patience was wearing thin as they worked on my face. For one, they were talking about me, my good looks in a disparaging manner. Secondly, the make-up was getting greasy in the heat and my face was itching. And last of all, the wig was too big and unwieldy.

So I was made two shades darker and the shooting began again.

But after the shooting of the initial scenes when the fifth time the director called for a halt, all hell broke loose. I threw my first and last star tantrum!

For this particular scene, they were to shoot me doing hard labour. Basically I was given a rag to clean the floor; I was supposed to be working at someone's home. And there was to be a close-up of my hands wiping the floor. That was when it happened.

Director: Action.

I start wiping the floor. Camera zooms in.

Director: Cut!

I look up surprised. Everyone looks up.

Assistant: Now what happened?

Director: She's got nail paint on. Look at her hands.

Assistant: Oh yes.

Oh yes, the vacations were on and my nails were painted a bright pink. So what?

Director: She's supposed to be a poor labourer; her hands should be dirty, rough. They can't be looking like this, all well-kempt. We need to take the nail paint off.

That was it! For the very first time during that shoot, I decided to not cooperate.

Me (with mutiny in my eyes): I won't take it off.

As the assistant came nearer, I said it a little louder.

Me: I won't take my nail paint off.

Assistant (in a tone of understanding): How will we shoot then?

Me: I won't shoot then. I won't take my nail paint off.

Director: See, *beta*...

Me (with shrill agitation): I won't. I won't. I won't. I won't. (Shrieking) AAAAAAI...

And I ran to my mum, sobbing. Everyone gathered around.

Assistant director: Come on *beta*. We'll buy you a chocolate.

Me: No!

A: Ice cream then?

Me: No!

Sob. Sob. Sob.

Director: See *beta*, you have been such a good girl. Just a bit of adjustment.

Me: No!

Make-up artist: We'll paint your nails again after the shoot.

Me: No!

Aai: Jaanu, just this once.

Me: No! No! No!

Cool. They didn't have all day and they had to shoot a lot of scenes. Of course, not shooting the hands was out of question. So they went ahead and shot my hands the way they were. Maybe they were pissed off with me, but the rest of my scenes were shot without further ado. My sad, sorrowful look was working for the mood.

When the make-up artist was removing my make-up after the shoot:

Make-up artist: Arre, you are *ekdum ek number star* (You're the top-rated star). What a tantrum you threw.

I was feeling terrible already. My eyes welled up with tears.

Make-up artist: Arre, don't cry. *Ekdum* Sridevi type of star you are. She also refuses to take off her nail paint.

Me (tearfully): Really?

Make-up artist: *Haan*. She refuses to look poor.

Me: Then. Who likes to look poor?

Make-up artist: Nobody does. But sometimes the role demands it na. Otherwise, how will you become an actress?

Me (with a sniff): I don't want to become an actress. See how I am looking? So ugly.

Make-up artist: Arre, don't worry. Nobody watches *Kamgar Vishwa*. Nobody will remember you like this.

That's true actually. Nobody really saw *Kamgar Vishwa* and the whole series ran and sank without a trace, thank God.

But that episode convinced me that I really never did want to act again. I did, of course, continue to perform on stage for the Stree Mukti Sanghatana, my school and in random acting workshops for quite a few years after that, but acting stopped being an aspiration. But this stint taught me a lot.

Most regular parents would have told their daughter to take the dismissal from the school play in their stride. The child would have been advised to not get disheartened, that the play was stupid and unimportant and to stop feeling so bad about it and forget about the whole thing. My parents, however, used this rejection to sharpen my focus on what I wanted and how I had to make it happen. They looked at how much acting mattered to me and they showed me how to fight for the things I wished for. That one single episode taught me to look at rejection very differently. Besides it took care of all my confidence issues forever. If you dream, you need to find the way to fulfil your dream as well. This life lesson, fortunately, is the only remnant of my acting aspirations.

# 13.

# When Life Throws You Limda

As life lessons go, Limda soap proved to be an important one. We loved our soaps in those days. They were the only whiff of fragrant extravagance for a generation which grew up without perfumes or deodorants.

That's why the memory of Limda is so important. Soaps are meant to be soft, squishy, yielding. Not Limda. Limda was green, tough and as unyielding as Mamata Banerjee. But to understand Limda, you need to understand those times and the place.

Vacations are tough on working moms, especially if they do not have a trusted maid to look after the child. Worst of all, even trusted maids go on month-long vacations during the summer. That puts a spanner in the works. My mum's solution to this problem was to courier me off to either Sucheta maushi's (her elder sister) in Grant Road – she was a lecturer in a college and had vacations too – or to Bharti kaki's (her sister-in-law) in Vasai. I must have spent more than three weeks at a go in each place every summer. Vasai was almost akin to a native place for me.

Bharti kaki lived in one of those big, big old houses in Bhaskar Alli (alley) in old Vasai. At the time, the big house was divided into three homes. Bharti kaki's brother, Dada mama (whose real name we did not know till he died; everyone called him Dada, even his own mother) and her mother, Chhoti aaji (whose real name I still do not know), lived in one set of flats on the ground floor. Her other very psycho brother and his psycho wife (who did not get along with Bharti kaki and her mother) and their two children lived in another flat. And Bharti kaki, Anna kaka (my father's older brother) and Ashwin dada (my cousin) lived on the top storey.

The house had high ceilings, a tricky wooden staircase, big photos of scary looking ancestors, glass eagle decanters, a small piano and a large terrace. It used to be a hospital at one time; Bharti kaki's father was the only doctor in Vasai for ages and his home was half hospital. Patients were admitted and treated here; relatives came and stayed with the patients and they paid for their treatment in whatever way they could. Some gave a room full of bananas, some supplied notebooks to last a couple of years, some offered a daughter or son in marriage. Student doctors came to study and lived in the house itself. Bharti kaki's mother apparently planned food for 40 people everyday.

Well, the house was magical and a bit scary for me as a child. It had a lot of trees around it and many places forbidden to us: a mango tree with a *munja* (the Konkani version of a ghost of an unmarried and therefore unhappy youth), a *raatrani* tree which rendered people unconscious with her fragrance and kidnapped them, a big attic from which emerged strange eerie sounds and a couple of rats, a deep well where evil spirits lurked, waiting to catch young girls leaning into the well for a look and a plot full of overgrowth in the backyard.

No doubt that it was the elder cousin, Ashwin dada, and his help, Sunil dada (a teenager who helped Bharti kaki around the house and played with us when he didn't have work or studies), who were making up these stories to spook me. There were very few streetlights and it would become dark very early and there were a lot of power cuts.

There were interesting characters around too, one of which was Dada mama.

He was a big fly in the ointment of Vasai. He loved to rile me. For some reason, he had a piano, although I never heard or saw him playing it. And he didn't allow us to use it. After my mother gave birth to Tanvi, my younger sister, he loved to tease me.

Once my father dropped me off in Vasai, Dada mama would start.

DM: So Jaanu, your father has left you here.

Me: Yes, for ten days. He'll come to pick me up.

DM: What if he never comes?

Me: Why will he do that?

DM: They have a new baby now. They may not want you anymore.

Me (warily): Of course they want me.

DM: Then why have they sent you away?

Me: Because we don't have anyone to take care of me when my mum and dad go to office.

DM: Ha. That's what you think. When you are not around, they will buy new clothes for Tanu. And new toys.

Me: No they won't.

DM: They will. Ask Bharti.

Me: Bharti kaki, will Aai-Baba buy new toys for Tanu when I am not there?

BK: No they won't. (To Dada mama) Dada, don't harass the poor child. She'll miss her parents and cry.

DM: Arre but it's true.

BK (taking me on her lap and holding me tight): Fine, if her parents do that, we'll buy Jaanu some toys over here. And if they don't come to take her, we'll enroll her in a school here and keep her with us.

Sometimes, he would tease me about the people living in my building. Once I was talking about Hamen, the Parsi boy who lived in the building next to ours and his mum Parveen.

DM: Parveen Babi lives in the building next to yours?

Me: Not Parveen Babi, just Parveen. She's Hamen's mum.

DM: There is no such thing as only Parveen. Only Parveen Babi, the actress.

Me: But she is not the actress.

DM: How do you know? What is her surname?

Me: I know. I don't know her surname.

DM: Ha. You know but you don't know. How can that be?

Me: Ohhhh, Bharti kaki, Dada mama is troubling me again.

BK: Dada, don't trouble her so much.

That man really had nothing to do and I long gave up trying to make the effort to like him. Once I complained to Bharti kaki about him.

Me: Why is your brother like this?

BK: Like what?

Me: So *kuchkat* ('rotten' in Marathi). He's always troubling me.

BK: But why do you pay any attention to him? Will your parents really leave you here?

Me: They won't. But then why does he say it?

BK: Arre, he only says it because he knows you always react like this.

Me: But if he says things like this, how should I react?

BK: Don't pay him any attention. I told you to leave the room when he starts talking to you.

Me: I do, but he follows me and keeps talking to me. How many times do I tell him to not talk to me? I don't like him. How can you like him?

BK: Dada, stop re. Don't you have anything better to do?

DM: But what have I done?

The other fly in the ointment was the big, fat, green lizard in the loo. Bharti kaki's home had a huge terrace and like all old places, the loo and bathroom were at the other end of this terrace. The bathroom had a dim light and the terrace had none. This meant that if you wanted to do *su-su* at night, you would have to walk through the terrace alone in the dark. This terrace had at least one frog, several lizards, caterpillars, millipedes and many inhabitants of the insect world. If one were to do a quick sprint, an encounter with any of them could be avoided. The loo, however, was a different case. It had a queen lizard. She was huge – at least as long as my hand – and three inches thick, uneasily green-yellow, with big, round, bulging eyes. And that chick was scared of nobody.

No amount of vibrations created by pounding a stick on the loo's wall or burning paper in the corner or stomping feet outside on the terrace (all Ashwin dada's ideas) could make her back off. We even tried crossing our eyes and threatening her, but to no effect. She would just stay stuck to the same spot on the left wall of the loo, right next to the zero bulb, glowing menacingly and gulping once in a while. I suspect she may even have rolled her eyes at our feeble efforts to get rid of her. What you cannot conquer, you need to learn to compromise with. And so, I developed a coping strategy:

Step 1. Hold the *su-su* for as long as one can.

Step 2. When absolutely uncontrollable, rush to the loo, gingerly push open the loo door with one finger and locate Queen Lizard.

Option 1. If not there, quickly do *su-su* and run out.

Option 2. If QL turns up stomping from the window, take that as the cue to discontinue the *su-su* and rush out anyway. (Frequent falling and tripping on the coba floor of the loo steps and terrace happened because of this.)

Option 3. More often than not, the lizard would be there, waiting silently with raised eyebrows or with a half-eaten cockroach sticking out of her mouth like a cigar. In which case, you cringe, slip sideways into the loo, start *su-su*, hoping that QL does not move, then sidle out silently and run for your life.

In those days, Vasai was at the forefront of research and development and experiments on insects and pest control technology. Ashwin dada particularly would pore over those Britannica-like books about insect species and devise ways to deal with them. This was the place where I learnt about *kachhwa chhaap* agarbatti, big mosquito nets under which I pretended to be a princess and the smelly Odomos, which I pretended was Afghan White Snow and lathered it all over my face and hands. This is where I learnt that sticking lit Diwali fire sparklers into the stems of household plants will cause caterpillars to crawl

LIMDA
LIMDA
LIMDA

down from the plants, get into your skirt and deposit their talons all over your thighs and legs, which then cause intense itching and need to be removed with pincers. Oh, and that Lacto Calamine and Boroline are the answer to all insect bites and sores.

This was where I saw and learnt to be wary of big beetle-like red ants, bright green staring frogs, silent and watchful cockroaches around the plants, and nail-like thorns that could pierce even slippers.

I also learnt the connection between *chuna* and mehendi, the various uses Dalda *dabbas* could be put to (Ashwin dada once put a bomb in it and lit it; only fragments of the tin remained), and of course, Limda.

See, the thing is Bharti kaki used to run a wholesale agency to sell food and household products for companies like Procter & Gamble. She had a big godown/office near Vasai station, laden with Noga jam and ketchup bottles, detergent packets, Vicks inhalers and Swad *churan* candy. I have spent many a day in that dingy godown when my cousin had tuitions (with the intimidating and dictatorial Dubey Sir). I would play detective, sifting through the rows of sacks or pretend to be a model and endorsed those products for the godown employees, who were forced to watch it only because I was the boss' niece.

Sometimes I would play with old challan books, pretending to be my kaki, asking why certain details or entries were not filled in the book or signing some random papers. Sometimes I would watch a truck unload the *maal* (goods), the stacking of the products and how the manager would check if everything was as per the order or see how many units were sold at a time.

Then at some point, the business folded up and Bharti kaki started a smaller version of that agency right at home. She hired salesgirls to go out everyday and sell items of daily use such as phenyl, bath soaps, home-made ketchup and jams, sanitary napkins, those fancy multi-purpose kitchen clamps, cloth dusters and so on. I would watch Bharti kaki teach the girls how to talk to customers, how to write out sales orders, what area to cover, and how to collect money from the sale.

A normal work meeting at the end of the day would go like this:

Kaki: So Pushpa, how was your day?

Pushpa (or Swati or Sushma): Phew, it is so hot. It was good. But that Joshi kaku is a *haraami*. When she meets me in the bazaar, she asks me to drop in. But when I do go to her place, she will just look at everything and do 'ooh-aah' and say, 'next time'.

Kaki: That's okay. She will buy next time. Not everybody will buy all the time. Did you go to that Pinky's house? She wanted some phenyl bottles, hair oil and liquid soap, she said.

Pushpa: *Haan*, I went. She took the stuff but she said she'll pay you later.

By then, some other Sushma or Usha would arrive.

Sushma: Hello madam.

Kaki: How was your day?

Sushma: Madam, you know Kulkarni's daughter-in-law is pregnant. It's been seven years since their marriage.

Kaki: That's good.

Sushma: Yes, their neighbour Desai is saying that they went to a baba, who held her wrist and gave her some fruit. She was at home for four weeks before they announced that she was pregnant. She's been wearing a stone also, they say. The baba has guaranteed it will be a son only.

Kaki: Where do you get all these stories?

Sushma: Arre, on the field.

Kaki: What have you sold today?

Sushma: Ten packets of naphthalene balls, three bottles of phenyl, one liquid soap. Madam, customers are complaining about the last stock of liquid soap. It doesn't foam at all. Hey Pushpa, do you have nail paint? Give me na.

Kaki: *Haan*, some others have complained too. We'll find out what's wrong.

Sushma (while applying nail paint): Arre, they do some mistake and we have to answer our customers. Madam, why don't we sell salwar kameezes and sarees and beauty products? It would be so exciting.

Kaki: Then you only would be buying your own products.

Pushpa: Yes and there would be fights about who would take the testers home. And Sushma would discuss how many pimples Joshi's daughter-in-law has after the pregnancy. Let's make tea.

Once, amid such general gossip, a consignment of Limda soap was delivered.

In those days, people had a different relationship with the soaps they used. That generation was not into brand promiscuity. Every family only ever used one kind of soap, although there were quite a few of them around. Aaji-Ajoba used Jai soap. It came in a shiny pink cover with *jaswand* flowers on it. Sucheta maushi's house always had a Liril or Lux, while we always had Rexona or Hamam soap, hard rectangles of solid green. On the first day of Diwali or on the occasion of a family wedding, with great fanfare, my mum would unwrap a Moti soap and then carefully put away the wrapper in her saree shelves. Every year, D'souza mama (Aai's friend who worked in the Gulf) brought us a white Lux or Camay. Till I was 10 or 12, we only ever used Tata shampoo in that curvy glass bottle. Every Sunday morning, Aai would take the yellow shampoo in a bowl, dilute it with some water and keep it on the bathroom shelf for all of us to use during our baths.

We were gentle, careful with our soaps. We used our soaps till they were such tiny, thin slivers that they could only be picked up with the nails or needed to be shifted around till they came to the edge of the soap dish so they could be lifted. When they became even smaller, they were stuck to the mass of leftover slivers of soaps meant to be used at the wash basin outside the loo. They were used till they all merged into a single rainbow.

Soap wrappers were never disposed of either. They were kept between rows of folded clothes in our cupboards or under some books in our book shelves or in the jewellery drawer or in pillow cases. Nazia's drawer always smelled of Hamam or Lux. And just sometimes, a wrapper would fall out of a crisp, ironed salwar kameez.

We didn't waste our soaps. Well, I did – once. In an bid to create vanishing cream (what that product made vanish I still do not know), I sneakily lathered a large part of a soap and collected the foam in a jar. Knowing Aai's reservations about some of my experiments, I hid the jar in the freezer. But that same evening, she found out.

Aai: Jaanu, what did you do with the soap?

Me (shrugging): Nothing. Why?

Aai: Do not lie.

Me: Nothing Aai. Why?

Aai: Then how come the soap has become so small?

Me: How do I know?

Aai, of course, believed that claiming innocence incriminated me further.

Aai (wagging a finger): Do not lie.

Me: God promise. (That was as popular as Hoppingo-Battingo in my day.)

Aai stares.

Aai: You think money grows on trees? That your father and I work so hard so that you can only waste things.

I give up.

Me: I did not waste the soap. I only used some of it.

Aai: You mean for a purpose that didn't involve bathing or washing?

Me: Hmm.

Aai: What?

Me: To make cold cream.

Aai: What!

Me (hurriedly): Meghna told me if you collect soap lather in a cold cream jar and put it in the freezer, it turns into cold cream.

Aai: So you wasted half a bar of soap? Is Meghna's father going to buy you a new soap?

Me (hopefully): Yes, but we don't need to buy cold cream then. So much *fayda*.

Aai: That Meghna is a fool and you don't have any brains of your own at all.

That jar of lather remained in the freezer for days. But it never turned into cold cream. Only for scientific reasons, if you are wondering what happens to soap lather when frozen, here is the answer: the lather vanishes and only iced water remains.

We respected our soaps. And that's why it was doubly hard to come to terms with Limda.

So what was so different about this soap, you ask? Different, in the sense that as products go, this one was an utter, abject failure. Soaps lather; Limda didn't. They are fragrant; Limda smelled of… well, nothing. But most importantly, basic to their nature, soaps dissolve when in contact with water; they dent when they are dropped. Not Limda. Limda didn't dissolve in contact with anything; it didn't give in to pressure, physical or emotional.

Limda was a neem soap. As it is, neem soaps are nothing to write home about. They are green and smell of whatever neem is supposed to smell of. So as a concept itself it was like say, Kumar Gaurav. I mean, given that he was biologically conceived by Rajendra Kumar itself limited his star potential somewhat. One couldn't expect him to be Amitabh, could one?

Like that fat, green lizard in Bharti Kaki's loo, Limda just sat there in her soap dish, staring at you, daring you to make an impression. The first time I used this soap, it perplexed me. As a child, hand-washing was never a priority, particularly in Bharti kaki's bathroom. I usually washed my hands in a jiffy and rushed out. In my innocence, I believed that all soaps (and humans too, I guess) did what they were supposed to do – fulfil their destiny and all that. However, Limda made me think again.

With my head turned and an eye on the lookout for the lizard or a cockroach, I turned on the tap and reached out for the soap. I rubbed my hands with the soap and kept it back, the water running all the time. No lather. That in itself was not unusual; Vasai did get hard water. I rubbed my hands together once more. No lather. I turned my head and looked at the soap. The water wasn't that hard. I rubbed this green soap on my hands again, harder. Some green colour rubbed off, but still no lather. Now I was intrigued. I rubbed and a lot more green colour came off. I got scared that I was wasting soap, quickly washed my hands and ran out to Bharti kaki.

Me: Bharti kaki, Bharti kaki. Look at my hands. Limda doesn't lather only.

Bharti kaki: Yes, I know.

Me: Why doesn't it lather?

BK: I don't know. I suppose it's defective. People are asking for refunds.

Me: Really? All those soaps we ordered?

BK (with a smile): Yes.

Me: All of them?

BK: Yes, all of them.

Me: So now?

BK: Nothing. It's defective. It can't be sold.

Me: Then why are we still using it?

BK: Because we have paid for it already as an agency. We can't ask for a refund.

Me: Arre, can't you just say that it's not a good soap and ask for your money back? Like all our customers did.

BK (smiles): No *baba*.

Me: So what do we do?

BK (cheerfully): Use the soap ourselves. Sometimes we have to live with the mistakes we make. Look at it this way, now we don't have to spend on soaps for a long time.

True. There was a serious amount of Limda out there, a tall stack of soap bars. Bharti kaki's business and household finances were in serious trouble. They had been for several years. Kaki hadn't been able to repay her business loans as easily as she had expected. But in her calm, stoic, dignified way, Bharti kaki only focused on how to make things work.

This is the woman whose whole life and house was crumbling around her but she still had the time to put mehendi on my hands or make *gajras* out of the flowers I collected from her garden. This is the woman who had a roomful of bad soap. But she never washed her hands off any of it.

She devised that only rubbing wouldn't melt Limda's heart. So she started soaking the bar in water; after some days, the green liquid soap was infinitely easier to pour into a palm and use, although it still didn't lather much. They used it like this for a really long time in the Vasai bathroom. It was a solution of sorts, but Bharti kaki wasn't interested in solutions. She wanted complete triumph.

After a few weeks, Bharti kaki started using this solution to even wash clothes. But that experiment failed: the clothes started turning slightly green. A few months later, Kaki decided that the enemy needed to be broken down bit by bit. So one afternoon, she sat with a scraper and grated a full bar of Limda, just like one grates cheese. She then put some of the *choora* into the soap bowl to wash dishes with. That household, and ours, washed a lot of dishes with this innovative soap *choora*.

It could have been used even as a foot scraper. And, I discovered later, for make-up purposes. Once I scrubbed the soap too hard on my cheeks to get it to lather. After I came out and checked in the mirror, I realised that my cheeks were really sore but also bright red. I realised that in lieu of rouge (Bharti kaki didn't wear any make-up; I had to use a sketch pen on my lips to paint them!), I could use Limda on my face. Of course, Aai didn't agree.

Once after I came out from the bathroom, my mother shrieked.

Aai: What happened to you?

Me: What?

Aai: Why is your face so red?

Me (excitedly): It looks just like rouge na? It's Limda. If you scrub it hard enough, it will make your cheeks go red. I'm looking so pretty.

Aai looked disbelieving.

Aai: What have you done?

Then she saw how sore my cheeks were; she gave me one whack.

Aai: *Deed-shahani* (oversmart). Who puts these ideas in your head? Come, put some cream on.

Me (affronted): It was my own discovery. I've such red cheeks now.

Aai: You are looking like a red-faced monkey. Now use some cream quickly before you spoil your good skin.

Over time, Ashwin dada devised a new use for the soap bar; it was used to stick mosquito coils or agarbattis in or to adjust uneven table legs.

"You're still using Limda?" I would ask in amazement every time I visited Vasai over the months. "Yes, what to do? We're poor people," Kaki would reply with a laugh, just as easily reaching for a Lux specially bought for me to use while I stayed there for a week.

Over the years, my visits became more and more infrequent, more rushed. Dada mama had passed away but there were still vacation classes, scholarship exams, board exams. Anna kaka passed away. Chhoti aaji passed away too.

The house structure was redeveloped; there is now a building. Strange people came and started living in the vaastu that Kaki and Dada were born and brought up in. Kaki's agency folded up.

At some point, the Limda stock got fully exhausted. Ashwin dada is still there, so are all the plants and the big dark well. There is no scary queen lizard there but there is a big, fat, wide-eyed frog lurking about in the bathroom passage these days. My aircraft engineer Dada designs wheelchairs in his pastime. His son tells my son about the ghosts in that well. Kaki still runs a business, now of orthopaedic aids and machines. Her house is still full of stock but this time there are boxes of crutches and neck braces lying around. We tease Kaki that like Limda, we'll have to use all those braces and walking aids if she doesn't manage to sell them! But none of us have forgotten the learning inherent in our Limda experience: when life throws Limda at you, crush it and make it work for you.

# 14.

# Faaltugiri and the Pre-teens

*Faaltugiri*. The first time I said it, it stunned my parents into silence. Whatever did it mean? It was not a cuss word; neither was it an official Marathi word. Well, there was *faaltu* – which means trivial or useless but in a rude sort of way – but what was this suffix, *faaltu-giri*? My parents thought they were maha-pandits of the Marathi language and literature. Well, they had never heard of *faaltugiri* till I said it. To be honest, even I had never heard of that word till earlier that week. I am not even sure if that is a Marathi word. It meant the business of doing *faaltu* things, of course, and it originated from Siddhesh Patil, the great then-bully of Loukik.

The building group, consisting of Siddhesh Patil, Saurabh and Shalaka (Pinky) Tendulkar and me, was playing *sakhali* (you know where one person runs after the others and catches people, who then hold hands and catch the rest till only one is left). Now, Siddhesh was known to cheat liberally while playing. For instance, when playing *pakda-pakdi* or *sakhali*, Saurabh touched his elbow and shouted, "Out." Siddhesh loudly protested, "Not out. You have only caught my elbow, not me." The point being that his elbow was somehow different from HIM as an entity. There ensued a fruitless metaphysical debate on what was ME and MY-NESS and other kinds of notions relating to self-identity and whether body parts were essentially a part of it, how parts of a body do not sum up to the whole and therefore, are not liable to be declared out in the game.

It was quite usual for Siddhesh to bust a game in order to avoid taking the 'den' (his turn to catch everyone else). And it would result in all the others ganging up against him whenever he did end up taking the den. So then when he was finally running after us, his foot touched Saurabh's while running and he shouted, "Out." This time Saurabh protested, "Not out. You didn't catch me, your foot did." Right away, Siddhesh retorted, "Huh, what is this *faaltugiri*?"

Saurabh immediately imploded, "What's that word? There is no such word." But to be honest, we were charmed by this brilliant word. It expressed so succinctly all our angst and frustration at the unfairness and injustice at all that happened around us. I don't know what happened to that game. But two days later when Baba made me pick up the mess Tanu made, I protested.

Me: This is total *faaltugiri*. Not fair. Why should I pick....

Baba: What? What is that word?

Me: Which? *Faaltugiri*?

Baba: Where did you hear it? There is no such word.

Me: Of course there is. *Faaltugiri* means when *faaltu* things happen; that you are doing *faaltu* things. Tanu's made that mess; if you make me pick that up, it is a *faaltu* thing to do.

Baba: Shut up. And pick it all up. There is no such word.

Me: There is.

I sorted out the mess but I knew that Baba had been disconcerted by the word. *Faaltu* was a crass word to him. It didn't sound cultured to him. He was quite finicky about language. He believed that our language shows our knowledge and culture. He would bristle at wrong pronunciations, incorrect grammar or phrases. Once Baba kicked up a fuss because our school teacher was conducting the parent-teacher meeting in Marathi.

Baba (interrupting the teacher mid-speech): Excuse me, why are you talking in Marathi? Isn't this an English-medium school?

Teacher (affronted): Why? Do you not understand Marathi?

Baba: The point is not whether I understand the language. This is an English school; you should be conducting your meeting in English.

Teacher (looking at other parents for support): Is there anybody who doesn't understand Marathi here?

Other parents looked here and there and, clearly because they didn't want to get into trouble, murmured that they had no problem.

Baba: But that's not the point.

One bored parent: What is your problem? Aren't you proud of Marathi language?

Baba: If you're so proud of Marathi, you should have put your child in a Marathi-medium school. I'm saying this for your own good. Teacher, please talk in English.

Clearly, the teacher was talking in Marathi because she couldn't talk fluently in English and none of the parents had complained so far because they weren't so hot about speaking in English themselves. So the meeting continued in apologetic faltering tones and the whole agenda for the meeting went for a toss.

So you can imagine what he must have felt about this *faaltu* addition to my vocabulary. My grandmother was another Sanskrit heroine, fussy about language and all. The usual *Subhashit* spouting (Sanskrit four-liner poetry about life wisdoms) oldie flipped when she heard my word and called me illiterate (while recalling some *subhashit* about donkeys and language and culture).

And so, like a new toy – noisy and irritating – I used the word all the time. You know how some people use 'awesome' or 'amazing' to describe some very ordinary, un-awesome or un-amazing things or how they start their sentences with a 'basically' or 'actually' for no reason? I did that with *faaltugiri*. Waiting for a bus, being punished, being made to pick up stuff, eating radish or brinjal, almost everything became *faaltugiri*. Then the suffix began to be attached to other words, like *idiot-giri, stupid-giri* and so on.

It was then that I understood the power of language and how I could use it successfully to negotiate with the parents. So much in the child-parent relationship is controlled by the choice of words. So much was conveyed not only through the meaning but also the tone. I always knew Baba was serious when he said, "Now" or when Aai said, "*Bagh ha* (Now look here)" in those ominous tones. They could have called us 'stupid' but they always said 'stooppid'; they called us '*bindok*' (brainless or literally, headless). 'Fine', when uttered like a full stop, never meant fine; 'okay', when said softly, was never okay. And '*thik ahe*' (it's okay) when said gently meant it was not at all *thik*.

*Faaltugiri* went a bit further. As a 10-year old, I liked the tone, the irreverence, the indifference, the hint of rudeness and vehemence inherent in that word. And it was just the beginning. I realised that these random words had the power to silence my parents.

'Yaar' was the first of my own artillery of words in my war with them. In one smooth swoop, 'yaar' brought the whole parent-child hierarchy crashing. It totally levelled us.

Baba: Jaanu, have you finished your homework? Start that right away.

Janu: Arre yaar... I am just reading this book...

Baba: Yaar? I am not your yaar… all these Hindi films are ruining your language.

I realised I could get my own way by deflecting their attention from the point being debated by making it a language issue.

Then came '*fulltoo*'. It was a superlative term of description and said with a lot of phonetic enthusiasm: *fulltoo* timepass, *fulltoo* mazaa, *fulltoo faaltu*, *fulltoo* serious, sometimes things were just plain *fulltoo*. Once I said, "*Fulltoo khali hota* hall (the hall was 'fully' empty)" and Baba just raised his eyebrows.

Later in the eighth standard came '*sahi hai*' (it's cool/impressive), courtesy classmate and spiritual guru Shruti Jawle, who brought the choicest of silly words to us. '*Sahi hai*' really confounded him.

Baba: Come and watch these Chinese gymnasts.

(It was a trendy thing in those days to watch pretty Russian or Chinese acrobats or gymnasts doing weird body twists and wriggling on video. The highlight was when those chicks would roll their bodies in impossible positions in which they made their toes touch their eyebrows or their chin touch their knees.)

Me: Wow. *Sahi hai.*

Baba: What? Why are you talking in Hindi?

Me (still engrossed in the circus): Who's talking in Hindi?

Baba: You. You just said *sahi hai*. That's Hindi.

Me: Tch. It's Marathi. It means that it's impressive.

Baba: It is Hindi and it means that it is right or correct.

Me: I know what it means in Hindi. This is its Marathi meaning.

I know. I was fibbing. But it was worth it to see the irritation on his face.

Baba (exploding): *Sahi* is not a Marathi word.

Me: It is. It is.

Baba: IT IS NOT.

Aai to Baba: Why are you reacting so much? She is an idiot, just riling you. Let her say it if she wants to.

I did want to. *Sahi hai* became an anthem, a badge. It quickly replaced 'wow', 'yay', 'fantastic' and 'superb' in our vocabulary. By this time, my parents had already disowned me from their linguistic heritage. They were not tolerant of my accidents with Marathi or English, of course. They kept correcting me. But they had long realised that they did not remain my only influences. I was learning my language from everyone and everywhere around me: from mentors Baban kaka and Jagan kaka, my classmate influencers Shweta Agaskar or Reshma Gujar, teachers, television, film posters, painted ads near railway tracks, and so on. But such is the parent-child relationship, that soon they relented, enough to try and use these words themselves.

Aai: Jaanu, I've bought you a dress. See if you like it?

Me: Wow, *masta*. It's nice.

Aai (feeling generous and with a wide smile): *Sahi*?

Me (hugging her in my delight): *Sahi mein dahi.*

According to Jawle, when something became even better than 'fantastic' or 'superb', '*sahi*' became '*sahi mein dahi*', said with joy and excitement, stressing on the '*hee*'.

But by then we had already moved on to other words, other ideas, other weapons: short forms.

Aai: Jaanu, is Tanu studying?

Me: No she is just doing TP.

Aai: What is that? Some new subject?

Me: TP. Timepass.

Aai: Why can't you just say timepass then?

Why? Because it sounded good, cool. This was the time of *Qayamat Se Qayamat Tak*. I mean, what fool would call it by its full name if one could call it QSQT? Anyway, DM for downmarket, DL for dirty looks; *pakau* and loser followed in quick succession and with immediate impact. By which time, my parents were already whimpering, lost for words of their own that they could throw at us. But even as I dust my hands with glee and satisfaction over those verbal victories, I realise that what goes around will come around. And so...

"Aai, you are just HDFC." My eight-year-old son and I were arguing over homework as usual. It stopped me in my verbal tirade. But I knew which way this conversation went.

Me (with a straight face): HDFC is the name of a bank.

Saad: LOL it. You don't know its real meaning. (In a whisper) HDFC means Half Dumb Full Crack. You don't know anything!

Baba would be glad. I smiled to myself, readying myself for a new innings of the language war.

# The New Beginning

Many many years later, Vasant passed away. He went just like that, without warning. The crowd at his funeral was exactly like the one during his funny charas episode. To be honest, Vasant wanted to donate his body to science. However, the women in his life became a little wimpy and decided on a traditional funeral. There was also the slight issue of last rites, for which Vasant should have had a son. Aai decided that being the eldest daughter, I should do the needful. It led to a hushed outburst when she declared this.

Uncle 1: How can a girl do the last rites?

Aunty 1: Girls aren't even allowed to enter the crematorium.

Tatya kaka: Thank your stars that they are at least doing the last rites. Abu wanted to donate his body to science. Better that the rites are done. At least Abu will be proud that his daughter did this.

That must have been one of the rare few religious rites that my family has ever followed. We conducted the third-day rites and the tenth-day rites. On the twelfth day, Aai, Nazi, my sister and I alongwith a dozen relatives, waited patiently inside the Loukik compound for the crow to fly down and touch the banana leaf which held the food offering. The spread had all the last rites' goodies: dal, chawal, *gawar bhaji*, kheer. To be honest, the crow showed no interest.

SUDOKU
SUDOKU

Close relatives of ours who were present started murmuring.

Aunt 1: Oh my, why isn't the crow touching the food? Chitra, say that you will get your daughters married on time. Abu must be worried about them.

Uncle 2: Hahaha, that is Abu's soul. It won't touch vegetarian food so fast. Put some fish in it.

Someone else suggested that we promise that we would go to the family deity's temple in Konkan or at least Siddhi Vinayak temple. Chitra promised none of this. We just cooled our heels till the crow touched the food reluctantly.

But later that evening, reflecting on the vast wastage of cooked rice and silliness of the rituals and the amount of time the crow took to touch the vegetarian offering, Aai decided that there would be no more mournful *shraadhs* for Vasant.

The next year, she offered a plate to the crow for Baba. Nazia coolly placed two pieces of fried *bombil* (Bombay Duck) on it. The crow took eight seconds to finish the plate and everyone, including the crow, was happy.

With an essential, volatile ingredient like Baba out, things have become much calmer at 1, Loukik. Bored of solving the daily crossword without any of Vasant's irritating intellectual inputs, Chitra has shifted to Sudoku after retirement. The rest of the time she entertains herself by either arguing with her grandchildren or cooking for them.

The more I think of my dad or look at my mum, the more I appreciate my crazy upbringing. My parents' dismissal of religion, irreverence for social prestige, their love for poetry, literature, knowledge and argument, the freedom of voicing our opinions, the humour and sarcasm that was ever-present in our household, their disregard for perfection but their obsession with persistence, their innate love for confrontation – all the behaviours that parents of my generation are now discouraged from practising – these have shaped our personalities and attitudes toward life.

The plastic bags that we greedily demanded as customers are now banned today and rightly so. But Loukik and its gullies and all that was special about those Gold Spot days – the humour and affection in the sarcasm of our parents' criticism, their silly but lovable foibles – still remain wrapped in that bubble.

As the world changes rapidly, life at 1, Loukik is a reminder that some things also remain the same, only if you care to seek that similarity. Walking down memory lane is easy when you actually live in the same gully for an entire lifetime.

I am 42 now. I moved out of Loukik after marriage, only to move back in with my family three years later, into Prabhu's flat, three storeys above 1, Loukik. And the *faaltugiri* continues.

The dharamshala has a television of its own but patients still knock on 1, Loukik for small favours like boiling eggs or grinding masalas or in recent times, to send or receive money wired by relatives through e-banking. For the lack of devotional TV programmes, the dharamshala now has an enthusiastic clerk who sings mournful devotional songs himself on the loudspeaker every evening.

The chawl women can still be witnessed dragging home an errant alcoholic husband from the desi daru bar. Young boys still hang around on footpaths to SMS their gully sweethearts.

Ganapati is still celebrated with great fanfare on our street and continues to be a hub for romance. The street screenings may have stopped but there is a rather lively record dance competition that is as entertaining. Our children love sneaking out for Ganapati darshan just for the prasad, exactly like we did in the past.

My kids while away time by climbing like monkeys up the security grill outside our entrance door and chatting with random passers-by who frequent the temple. They find it funny that their mother is called 'baby' by shopkeepers and residents on the street. My son Saad saw Prabhu Deva dancing in a film and decided that he wanted to go 'inside' the film and dance. My daughter Saraa runs only on diagonal or alternate tiles and niece Vinni dances in front of the mirror and experiments with make-up. And all three of have started showing immense interest in watching drunken brawls on the street at night.

Mummyji still whiles away her day on the footpath outside her chawl and the Naidus have added a dozen grandchildren to their ilk in the last three decades. The Maharashtrian Baban kaka has been replaced by a UP *bhaiyya* called Chhotelal Kanojia, who now does *katti-batti* with the five-year-old Saraa through our window.

Ranjit Studio is no longer the landmark of our locality. The cycle rentals, the car garage have all been cleared off the streets. The junior artists, the saloons, the studios have all faded out. Dadasaheb Phalke Road now gleams with the finery of designer sarees in every garish colour possible. The few old shops that have managed to survive continue to thrive, despite rude salesmen.

A few years ago, I was at the Kamgar Grahak Shop on the main street with the son. This used to be a rationing outlet in the '80s and '90s and has now turned into a consumer cooperative shop. The salesmen here, Shivaji and his sidekick who we call Tanaji because we don't know his real name, are used to snapping at customers.

Me: That jaggery you gave me last week had ants all over it.

Shivaji (humorously): Baby, that is a special scheme. With 1 kg jaggery, you will get half kg ants free. Don't complain. That day your biryani got spoiled, you blamed the rice. (Then spotting my son, hiding shyly behind me) You, come, come. Shah Rukh Khan.

Saad (bashfully): No. I am Saad… not Shah Rukh Khan.

Shivaji: You don't like Shah Rukh?

Saad: No. I like only Salman Khan. (Then jumps up and starts an imaginary fight with someone.)

Shivaji: Oye Salman Khan, make sure you don't drop any of our stuff.

I absent-mindedly swatted Saad's hand as he flung the rice grains in the air, sighed and got on with my buying, suddenly reminded of Damu kaka's *khatmal ki chutney* and my acting. I knew Shivaji will completely disregard my preference and hand over a chocolate to Saad when we leave.

I am old enough to understand that that chocolate is more valuable than a thousand reward points and cashback that my credit card or the nearest mall will ever give me. After all, at times the salesmen in Kamgar Grahak also pay my fare if I suddenly find myself without a wallet when alighting from a taxi near home.

These are the few things that I hold on to in my fast-changing world. In a way, so much has changed and so rapidly for my generation. We have lived through the onset of the TV, the popularity of the video, the emancipation of liberalisation, the floppy discs and the compact discs, the proliferation of satellite TV, the Internet boom, the early mobile phones and then the smartphones, first the laptops and then the tablets, the video-calling, video-on-demand, and the now indispensable social media. Every three years, my generation has grappled with a new socio-cultural paradigm.

Today, it's all about making every second count, making every minute meaningful. My generation has the means to document every little thing we eat and live and breathe every minute. Every moment in our present can be captured and broadcast to the world. And yet our pasts – all the meaningless activities that nourished our souls, all the boredom that fed our intellect – are a complete haze. As we step into middle age, it's time for my generation to sift through our own flashbacks and figure out all the *faaltugiri* that enriched our own pasts.

# Acknowledgements

Inspired by Saad, Vinni and Saraa

Heartfelt gratitude to Aai, Baba and Nazi for just about everything.
A huge shoutout to my beloved sister, Tanu Rani,
such a big part of the book but not quite inside it.
And a million thanks to all those who have always believed
in me and my voice.